the sound of memory

MACHETE

Joy Castro, Series Editor

the sound of memory

THEMES FROM A
VIOLINIST'S LIFE

Rebecca Fischer

MAD CREEK BOOKS, AN IMPRINT OF
THE OHIO STATE UNIVERSITY PRESS
COLUMBUS

Library of Congress Cataloging-in-Publication Data
Names: Fischer, Rebecca (Violinist), author.
Title: The sound of memory : themes from a violinist's life / Rebecca Fischer.
Other titles: Machete.
Description: Columbus : Mad Creek Books, an imprint of The Ohio State University
    Press, [2022] | Series: Machete | Summary: "Personal essays on the life of a
    performing concert violinist in the twenty-first century, motherhood and
    musicianship, and the complexities of inheriting and passing down artistry"—
    Provided by publisher.
Identifiers: LCCN 2021046628 | ISBN 9780814258224 (trade paperback) | ISBN
    0814258220 (trade paperback) | ISBN 9780814281956 (ebook) | ISBN 0814281958
    (ebook)
Subjects: LCSH: Fischer, Rebecca (Violinist) | Women violinists—United States—
    Biography. | Violinists—United States—Biography. | LCGFT: Autobiographies.
Classification: LCC ML418.F57 A3 2022 | DDC 787.2092 [B]—dc23
LC record available at https://lccn.loc.gov/2021046628

Cover design by Regina Starace
Text design by Juliet Williams
Type set in Adobe Garamond Pro

for A, O, and I

contents

the family business

I wake up in bed, my head resting on a few books. The shadows have lengthened across the floor—it must be almost evening. I have fallen asleep again after school. I try rolling over to stretch, but I am met with something more than a post-nap stupor; it is envelopment in the sensation of being protected. Soft, percussive sounds float up the staircase. My mother is practicing the piano downstairs. She plays at all times of the day and night, whenever she can find a few minutes. Perhaps it's the music that's making me feel so soothed. Whatever she practices is a part of me, like patterns of breath.

I tug myself out of bed and head down the steps. The odd feeling persists; in fact, it intensifies as I pause on the wooden staircase. My mother's sound is warm, her playing is spacious and lyrical. She is engrossed in the music, then stands up quickly, her eyes on my glazed expression. "Oh, I didn't see you there. Are you ok?" I tell her I am having something like an out-of-body experience and wonder if it might be associated with the music. She is quiet for a moment. "I haven't practiced this piece in many years," she muses, then smiles. "You know, the last time I played this particular Bach Prelude was when I was eight months pregnant with you."

———⟋ꝰ

My family's material of choice is sound. Almost every one of my family members is a musician in some way. Character, color, flow, phrasing—these are our tools. Although sound can be measured, as a property it is unseen. Its waves and vibrations move through us, often finding a home.

Sound has sculpted my life as much as any tangible experience. I have often wondered if "rolling the tapes"—my mother's term for the automatic repetition of observed and learned family behavior—has led me to settle into my family's business. Is the depth of sound that I seek in my violin playing explained by growing up around my father's low cello sound and baritone voice; my sense of lyricism attributed to my mother's piano playing? How is my musical heritage an advantage, and how is it a limitation?

———⟋ꝰ

I look up in surprise at the podium. As concertmaster, my job is to work with the conductor to communicate phrasing, style, and tempo to the orchestra. But right away I can tell that the conductor's tempo is far too brisk; it is marching away from me. I have never played Ludwig van Beethoven's Seventh Symphony before, but something inside is pulling me slower. I try my best to keep up with the conductor, but it is miserable. I drag behind the rest of the orchestra, almost out of control. Afterwards I hurry home, upset by my inflexibility. My whole body is tense and I am trying to figure out why.

Later that night my parents offer a curious explanation for that afternoon: while preparing for my birth many years before, they took Lamaze breathing classes to help with the stages of labor, practicing their breathing to a mix tape. For one of the early stages, they selected the slowest recording they could find of the second movement of Beethoven's

Seventh Symphony, a live performance from the 1975 Marlboro Music Festival. My strong reaction to the orchestra that day was likely due to an opinion of tempo and pace developed before I was born.

———~♪

I was first introduced to the study of epigenetics when a friend mentioned it in passing after reading an article on his phone. "Finally," he said, "an answer to why my relatives hoard money and don't eat: epigenetics." I looked up at him from eating my lunch. "My grandparents," he explained, "almost starved in the Great Depression and trained themselves to survive on nothing. Maybe that's why I can go without food for long periods of time."

The theory behind epigenetics—the prefix "epi," in this sense, means "on top of" or "in addition to"—is that an individual's genetic makeup can be altered because of their parents' and/or grandparents' unique life experiences. This could be a passing down of the ability to handle stress, for example, or more likely, the inhibition of a hormone such as cortisol to battle stress, due to relatives' prior trauma. Changed genetic expression showcases patterns in families with similar life experiences.

I struggled as I tried to apply this information to my life. Perhaps I was destined from the beginning, through no plan or choice of mine, to pursue music. Could the genetics of sound entirely explain my narrative?

———~♪

My mother's mother was the first. At a young age, she showed talent and aptitude on the piano, both in jazz and classical performance. At sixteen she left her Oregon home to study at The Juilliard School in New York. While playing and singing at a summer stock theater production of a Gilbert and Sullivan operetta, she fell in love with a man five years her senior who sang the baritone roles. They married soon afterwards. That man—my grandfather, a scholar and linguist—went into the military and later the foreign service, and my mother's family moved around the world for his assignments.

My grandmother was proud of her vocation and enjoyed being the new face in a community. For her, the occupation of an artist was a position of service. Her own mother had been a doctor, a rare profession for a woman at the beginning of the twentieth century. While living in Nairobi, Kenya, for three years, my grandmother worked with two other musicians—a Russian violinist and a German cellist—to start a music conservatory, all while their trio toured and concertized. When the National Cathedral in Nairobi needed an organist, my grandmother learned how to play the instrument on the job. In other locations—Karachi, Pakistan; Arlington, Virginia; Hong Kong; Lawrenceville, New Jersey—she stepped in to improvise for dance classes, teach the piano, and play recitals with local musicians.

I associate my grandmother with spontaneity, invention, and a deep alto voice with wide vibrato. When we arrived at my grandparents' place for vacation, my sister and I would run downstairs to the music room where my grandmother handed us percussion instruments from her travels—maracas, drums, cymbals. Leading from the piano, she would commence with our "Thanksgiving Jam" or "Ode to Spring Break," whatever celebrated the season. The improvisations themselves are unmemorable, but I can still hear her voice resonating throughout the household.

My mother says that her own musical path felt more predetermined than my grandmother's. As her mother's daughter she never expressed a particular zeal to be a musician—she just *was* a musi-cian. Everyone in her family, including her brother, a French horn player, practiced and performed regularly. Although my grand-father was not a professional, he sang for limited engagements and directed the choir at the National Cathedral in Nairobi. So it came as a surprise when my grandmother, by all appearances the upholder of the musical structures, found out that my mother was seriously involved with a cellist at Oberlin College planning to start a string quartet, and she didn't hide her dismay that he was a musician. Perhaps she was concerned about my mother's financial stability. Or perhaps she was skeptical of something else; it is hard to know. But that cellist, my father, was so ambitious and genially disarming that my grandmother eventually released her concerns.

Like my mother, I had no choice but to be around music. It was everywhere in my life, and nothing was ever done halfway in my house. We practiced at all times of the day; my father rehearsed long hours with his string quartet when they weren't on tour; stu-dents of my parents stayed at our house while babysitting me and my sister; musicians from all over the world came over for dinner parties that went late into the night. In this immersion, I devel-oped a strong sense of what a life in the classical music profession might be like.

I also gathered strong profiles of sound in my insides, only apparent to me when I began to play instruments. Were these expectations something I could attribute to nature or nurture, or a combination of both? Perhaps my sound was indeed a byproduct of generations of expression. What experiences of expression lin-gered in me, as apparent as bushy eyebrows or athletic ability?

—⁓

I vibrate the long, high note as delicately as possible, holding on like the end of a whisper. The second violinist and the cellists pluck their notes together, and the violists look up at me with faint smiles as they prepare to start their meandering melody. This musical transition feels like stepping into a magical garden, every time.

I watched my father and his friends rehearse this same music, years earlier. I was supposed to be doing schoolwork, but instead I sat absorbed in their playing. I marveled at the way these six musicians worked to sculpt every moment with sound, time, and inflection. They played it over and over again, the ethereal 2nd Adagio of the slow movement of Johannes Brahms's G Major Sextet. Sometimes the first violinist closed his eyes, seemingly lost in the music.

As I pass my own notes to the second cellist, I am also taken up with the music's dance. In this music there are no limits.

———

For me, it started with forced piano study. My musical parents thought it would be wise if I knew how to play such a versatile instrument. They got me lessons at the age of four, but I held no sustained love for the piano. I associated the instrument with obligation and being teased for leaving school lunch to practice. Playing the piano was only enjoyable for me when I gazed out of the window with melancholy in the midst of Frédéric Chopin.

I began studying the violin as a seven-year-old at a music program in my Vermont town. I was fascinated by the high, ringing register of the violin, and relieved to finally be able to sing on an instrument. At home I barricaded myself in my room, doling out mean-spirited glares to anyone who interrupted my work. It was often unbearably loud in our house with everyone singing and practicing, and I wanted my own space. Here I experimented with sound possibilities—richness, thinness, vibrato, no vibrato, brightness, paleness—trying to create the sound that was so clear in my head. Sometimes I cried when I played out of tune; I knew what beautiful intonation sounded like but couldn't yet achieve it. So I practiced and practiced, and I improved. With the violin and bow in my hands I answered to no one.

I knew at this young age that I loved music. I could even see myself playing the violin for the rest of my life—a gift of my upbringing: my parents modeled a fulfilling life in music. But I also knew that musical work took all of my family members' time and energy, and I feared it would envelop me completely. Life was work, and work was life. All children critique their family's professions, but I knew I had to keep one foot out of the door with music in case I fell too far in. As a child I spent more time drawing, writing, and reading than playing music, and I told everyone I would be a visual artist when I grew up. When musical activities dominated my schedule in high school, I often stayed up until 3 or 4 a.m. painting and reading in order to nurture these other passions of mine.

At extended family gatherings on both sides of my family, the younger generations were sometimes asked to play on command. When I stood up to perform in the midst of aunts and uncles, grandparents and cousins, I twitched with nerves. We were all fortunate to be able to play an instrument, so I know I should have been happy to share what I was studying, but I didn't see it that way. I was afraid of being judged. If the performance went well, I would be just another check mark in a family that expected greatness; if the performance went poorly, I would be thought of as a disappointment. My family did not set up this binary outcome based on our performances, but I still feared the possibility.

I did wish to share, to bring family members into my quieter expression. I would have been happier to play a personal concert for each of them, to discuss the musical mysteries that I was discovering alone while practicing. But that kind of exploration was impossible in a large group, so instead I bowed my head and waited my turn to play.

When it came time for me to go to college, I decided against attending a music conservatory full-time. Music-only environments, however welcoming, made me feel trapped. While studying philosophy, literature, and religion at a university alongside music, I routinely introduced myself to musicians without my last name, just in case they would regard me differently if they knew any of my relatives. My paranoia extended to summer music festival assignments—was I placed in leadership positions because someone knew my parents, or did I play well enough to earn it on my own? Friends from non-musical families said they wished they had been born into a musical family like mine, but I wondered what life was like in a family without any point of reference for what I did.

After I had been working in the music world for a few years, I heard an older musician say of me, "I see she got the teaching gene." I was flattered because I had measured up to one of my family's highest values, being devoted teachers and mentors. But then I wondered what would have happened if I wasn't interested in teaching. Would that same person have said the opposite of me— "Too bad she didn't get the teaching gene"? I wanted to create support and room for new expression of our family traits.

———

Another strong kick from inside my belly. She is awake. I can't move from my seat in the front row, so I settle in for the ride ahead. The first movement ends, and the minuet begins. My child is moving with the energy of the music being performed only thirty feet away. As the third movement of Ludwig van Beethoven's quartet Op. 18, No. 5 increases in intensity, the Takacs String Quartet's energy rises, and fireworks start going off inside of me. I muffle my laughter at the atomized popcorn exploding with every one of my baby's movements throughout the Beethoven, known informally as the "circus variations." I sneak a side glance at my friend sitting beside me. Surely she can see the aggressiveness of my baby's excitement. Wild motions adjust the fabric of my loose-fitting top. I breathe deeply and put my hand on my belly. A few weeks earlier I noticed her strong responses in my string quartet rehearsals to the drum-like beats of a Dmitry Shostakovich quartet. There is no choice but to join in—it is her home.

———

Upon receiving her first instrument my child's bright eyes opened wide, and she became silent. Then, slowly, she picked up the doll-like sixteenth-sized violin, raised it in the air and said, "Now we can play string quartets!" We all laughed, but I was uneasy. At the age of three she had begged to start learning the violin and I had impulsively said no. Initially this was for protective reasons. I thought of playing auditions for committees made up of at least one person who knew my parents; their expectations, real or imagined, had caused me to shrink. A small part of me had also wanted for our nuclear family to break the generations-long cycle of holding a place in the music world. I wanted to shield my eager child from the complexity of a musical life.

We were embarking upon a fourth generation of musical study, and my child was likely to do extremely well. She saw what it took to work hard, she had a great ear, and she possessed the temperament of a performer. Even as a four-year-old the sound she made on the violin was substantive—solid, rich, and warm. Her control in the early stages of learning was purposeful and confident. Was this a family sound showing itself in yet another generation? Maybe she would, like me, also wrestle with the gift of her genetic inheritance.

My grandmother's concern about her own child's musical future felt close at that moment. Maybe I had unfairly judged her worry about my mother entering a musician's life. It made perfect sense for children of musicians to pursue a career they knew. My child grew up in a house where art, writing, and music were what you spent your time doing. One of the questions she asked her friends at preschool was "What quartet is *your* mom in?"

Then it happened again. We tried to steer our second child towards other instruments, but when we recommended the cello at the dinner table one night when they were two, they looked at us with horror and started sobbing. Just the day before they had marched into their sibling's room carrying a red plastic toy violin, declaring with immense pride, "I pay vi-o-YIN!" For the next few years they studied the violin "just like mama" and their sibling—it was what the musicians in the house did. But they didn't seem to have a strong connection to the instrument. The violin didn't pull them in.

What carries each player towards their instrument? It is hard to say. Perhaps the bright pluck of a string or the clear echo of a wind instrument. At the age of six my younger child heard a flute performance and was transfixed. A sound was calling to them, even though they didn't have the words to say this at the time. The next day they spent hours and hours playing a flute head joint. They kept at that small piece of metal until they achieved the resonance they were seeking. I heard it right away when they found it; it was wholly theirs, and yet, familiar. As a mother and as a musician I knew this was their voice. No one else in our immediate family had been compelled to blow air through a tube. Their unique, lyrical sound seemed to be waiting in the instrument to be brought to life.

———⌐ꝰ

My sister's soprano voice shares a kind of resonance with my aunt's voice. My younger child moves their body with a sweep akin to mine. Now that my older child plays the viola, I detect a hint of my grandmother's alto sound in her lush viola vibrato. These kinds of cross-generational resonances are immediately apparent when our family meets for chamber music readings on holidays. Inherent in our collaboration is an understanding that doesn't need to be analyzed, an ease that does not need to be discussed. In my family's portrait of sound, I hear the aural equivalent of a physical trait like a smile winding its way through generations.

But this gift of resonance, a hallmark of a musical family's genetic expression, only grows when we recognize its wideness. When we hear this sound's openness; when we are guided by our children's freedoms, their practices, their questions; then the wideness is able to flourish. When we lean in too hard, our children's expressive freedom is lost. It becomes forced, too close.

My children's expression may resemble mine in look and sound, but it is not mine, thankfully. Their experiments may break apart whatever solutions I have found. As they sing, as they write, as they strike and coax sound out of wooden and metal containers or giant boxes with hammers and strings, they question what a life in music is and could be.

They may, like my grandmother, my mother, and myself, find pride in their identity as musicians. They may decide, like me, that music cannot be everything, even if they choose it as a career. They may decide that music will play only a tangential role in their lives. They may also recognize that music is a part of their breath and motion. In looking to the future, I think of my grandmother's example, two generations before me: let life be improvised, full, and sung.

Corpus Christi

Body and blood; body and milk. Milk that won't stop. Not just during the day, not just when pulling off to the side of the road to satisfy my baby's hunger, but every two to three hours my breasts swell to capacity. Down in Corpus to perform with my quartet, I know it is time when the familiar tightness arrives in the midst of rehearsal, at a restaurant table, or in the early morning hours. My body is beautifully connected to my child's needs. My produce is in demand, and I meet it. Everything else is secondary. In the middle of the night I finish feeding my child and fall back on the hotel pillows, hearing music in my head that I will play tomorrow, practicing in between states of consciousness.

We are three hours into the trip when I wake up from dozing and hear my nine-week-old child fussing and licking her hands. She has been sleeping next to me in the back seat, lulled by the car's motion for a longer-than-usual nap, but now she makes her presence known. Part-murmuring, part-sniffling, she pummels her face with her tiny fists, back and forth. She is not yet quite old enough to stare me down, but when I lean into the car seat and whisper, "Hi there, little one," she looks around wildly and launches into a scream. Despair, terror, the world could end for that cry.

My friend drives speedily in the stifling temperature, the heat threatening to melt the concrete. We are on a mission: battling time for someone else's needs. But my child is ready. We pull off to the side of the road and keep the car on for the air conditioning as I prepare my baby to eat. I unbuckle the straps and take her carefully out of the car seat. As I unfasten my nursing top she is inconsolable. She writhes and searches for sustenance. She finds one breast and starts gulping. The car is silent except for her sucking and sighs.

I can tell we are close to Corpus because of the proximity to the sea. We have stopped in the area of marshland preceding Corpus's notorious factories, which loom ominously in the distance. The marsh grasses lie in patches between the pools of water. The land looks permanently flooded. When approaching from the north at nighttime, a "city" of lights is visible for miles on the horizon. We anticipate a real destination, a Texan Emerald City, then closer to the light source we realize it is an immense factory complex. The industrial buildings are morose kingdoms, towers and all, amidst the Gulf waters and weeds. I spot them in the distance out of the front window as I look up from nursing my child.

When my baby is done, I buckle her back into the car seat, her wide eyes now warm and calm. Getting out of the car to stretch, I am hit with a wall of familiar coastal humidity. We are miles away, but I catch a whiff of the garbage air. The nearby sea covers up pollution's stain for now.

———⁊⁓

Corpus Christi translates from Latin to "Body of Christ." Designating a location, no matter how devout the explorer, as the Body of Christ, holds it to a high theological expectation but also raises questions. What relationship does the naming of the city, colloquially shortened to "Corpus," have to do with its current state, what the city cares about, who lives there? How might the body figure into the city and its residents' lives?

The city of Corpus Christi, Texas, is said to have been named by Alonso Àlvarez de Pineda, a Spanish explorer known for drawing up the first map of the Texas coastline. He arrived at the bay on the feast day of Corpus Christi. Like other colonial tales, the foreign group assumed the authority to claim ownership and the naming rights. We will never know what the Indigenous inhabitants, in this case the Karankawa Native people, might have already been calling the semi-tropical region.

Like other South Texan coastal towns, this "Sparkling City by the Sea" is alluring to tourists. Residents' oceanside pace of life is leisurely. But Corpus's history is also full of violence and disappointment; havoc by hurricanes; bungled attempts to convert Indigenous peoples to a European diet, customs, and religion; and the challenges of establishing a vibrant port close to Mexico. It is the American Southwest after all. As far as I can read, the city of Corpus does not reveal a penchant for rituals, for the glorification of the body in general, or for possessing a predominantly Christian culture.

As a former Episcopalian, I have taken Communion many times, and I know the importance of being served the body and blood of Christ, one of the Catholic Church's holy sacraments. The quality of the blood (wine) and body (bread, or more often, wafers) can influence one's ability to enter into a reverent place.

The presence of Christ's body is easier to conjure in a monastery where hearty bread is baked daily and one receives it kneeling on a stone floor while monks are chanting, than standing in a new-fangled church holding a tasteless wafer while a band plays praise music. This religious ritual, no matter the earthly materials, always required for me the most imagination. Simply walking up to the altar and receiving wasn't enough—I had to engage with proper solemnity. What could be more sacred and harder to enter into?

—⟶

The body—of the body. The connection between the body and mind. The body's mind. The word *somatic* addresses this body-mind integration. A somatic assessment of an injury is holistic and includes the psychology surrounding the injury (i.e., my wrist is not healing because I hold unresolved anger at my parents for forcing me to become a tennis professional). A medical assessment might treat the physical pain with pills directed at that specific body part, while ignoring the larger picture. My own definition of *somatic* might be something like "the body's mind in communion with the physical."

Our bodies, as spaces, have the extraordinary ability to hold memories. Rooms, as another kind of space, carry unique energy in more abstract ways. I can enter a venue where I have performed and feel echoes of my past activity. Weill Hall at Carnegie Hall, for example, holds overwhelming energetic moments and tensions. So many musicians have had their professional debuts in Weill; people's careers have been "made"; nerves have risen sky high. A history of meaning is sensed in the seats of the hall, and in the anticipation backstage. I have played well in Weill, and also not so well. I remember each performance in that hall in a finite way, in addition to what transpired afterwards, the reviews that came in, the comments I received.

In contrast, I can breathe with ease in the Troy Savings Bank Music Hall in Troy, New York. The warmth of the space's sound and the tilted wooden stage instantly evoke my creativity, as I spent many hours recording string quartet albums there. One feels the sincerity of the music made in that hall above a bank, a frequented tour spot in the 1900s for the world's greatest artists. Both halls carry their occupants' distinct memories.

My body knows its history in ways that defy rationalization. I attempt to be guided by my body's instincts, even though I cannot always seem to listen. Playing a musical instrument involves an immense amount of nuance and attention to detail, and honing my skills of observation is an essential part of being a musician. I know that I have to stop playing if my shoulder hurts in the practice room—my body gives me that familiar warning sign. But if I fail to respond, if I push through, the next day I suffer strain that could have been prevented had I listened.

I come back to music I haven't played since I was young, and my body remembers how I used to play it; my arms, fingers, and posture take on the habits of a younger person. Unless I cultivate a new relationship to the piece with my more efficient, updated technique, my body will continue to perform what it remembers. All artists are forced to wrangle with past and present vulnerabilities. We hold our memories close.

———⁓੭

Body and energy; a body's tremble. My first time in Corpus, and I'm shaking. I stand holding my violin, waiting for the pianist to get her pages settled. I can't look out at the audience, it's too much. I force the tip of my bow on the string to control my light convulsions and listen for the short piano introduction to the Mendelssohn Violin Concerto. My start to the piece is adequate, my sound better than I thought it would be. I might even appear stable, but I know it's fake confidence. This is only survival. Why can't I relax? I try to stay focused on my playing, but I keep wondering: after all of this, will they regret choosing me?

I moved to Houston, Texas, as a junior in high school. We relocated for my parents' work, but the move felt to my sensitive teenage spirit like a gift. We had been living in a small college town in Ohio in which I was faltering. The lake effect cloudiness made me listless, and I had few friends my age who were also pursuing music. Even though I was a diligent student of the violin and school, all of my work seemed to evaporate right after I completed it. I passed out of high school French classes, enabling me to take a language course at the local college, but afterwards I hardly ever returned to my high school. I took long walks around the town instead. My second semester of sophomore year I was marked absent forty times. Depressed, I agreed with my parents that leaving home for an arts-focused boarding school was a wise idea.

Our move to Houston allowed me to enroll in an arts-focused public high school ten minutes from my house. In the warm Texan environment, my mental health improved. I walked at all hours of the day and night in the humid air and danced in the tropical rainstorms. I practiced violin in my sunlight-filled room, a space that also inspired late-night watercolor painting sessions. My violin teacher, who had also moved to Houston, said she was relieved I had found myself again.

I was more committed to music than ever, practicing three to four hours every day on top of chamber music and orchestra rehearsals. In Ohio I had noticed that the harder I worked towards a performance the higher my stakes became, and my nerves increased. My stage fright symptoms were similar to other people's: body shakes, cold and clammy hands, difficulty seeing the larger picture when onstage. Now that I was happier in Houston, I lost some of my performance anxiety, but I still had to expect the shaking. I worried that more devoted preparation would provoke debilitating nerves.

In the spring of my junior year, I drove down to Corpus to compete in the Corpus Christi High School Competition. We arrived to the smell of mold in our hotel, the kind of wet thickness you wish you could exit. I found reprieve from it only when walking a few blocks to the sea. Corpus as a place had initially meant nothing to me apart from the competition. However charming, it was just another city in a wild state to which my family had moved earlier that year.

During the final round of the competition, I played with poise and accuracy. After many months of work, here was the performance I had prepared to give. I danced onstage with my violin, I sang, and I didn't shake at all. But when I heard I had won the string division and was now expected to perform again for the winners' concert, after which the jury would select the recipient of the grand prize, I froze. How could I recreate that peak performance?

Tightness built in my limbs as I prepared for the concert in the rooms of Corpus's Del Mar College. I was proud of being heard and recognized earlier that day, but I wasn't prepared for the torrent of energy that followed; physical joy moved to dread. My body's natural flow was trapped in a set of erratic fits and bursts.

The performance passed by without terrible incident, but after the competition I associated Corpus with a new awareness. Trust and fear were equally present inside of me, and I had begun to reckon with both of them. For the first time I acknowledged how integrated my entire body felt when playing my best, as well as how the currents of my nervous system could throw me off. In Corpus I saw that I had hope of a choice when faced with fear onstage. I suppose my body still retains this somatic lesson.

———

Body and milk; liberation and mourning. I have packed my hand breast pump to keep milk production up, just in case. Both children are at home. I know I will follow the timing of my second child's one short feeding, but I also know that this part of our relationship is over. It is now time to recover my body. How has my creative expression changed while learning to take care of other people? Can I find a new patience for myself?

I stand by the sink in the dimly lit, yellow bathroom of the Corpus Christi Holiday Inn and hand-pump from my one breast still producing milk. The small amount of warm, fresh liquid disappears down the sink drain as I dump out the bottle. While drawing out the last bit of sustenance from a body used lovingly and willingly for children, I wonder: what is gained and what is lost?

The day was chilly for south Texas. The wind ruffled the paper napkins on our outdoor table and threatened to overturn our basket of chips. My colleague and I had stopped for a meal in San Antonio on our way down to Corpus. As my hair whipped around my face,

I felt both excited and guilty for my bodily lightness. Breastfeeding had been a comforting reality in my life, not a burden. But now that it was no longer present, I didn't know why I felt so free. The ending of this kind of maternal relationship with my child had seemed right at the time of the decision, but it was also bittersweet. Would they still want to bond with me when I returned? Would I now become like any other person in their life, someone who had never shared a body-sustenance connection?

Pumping milk in strange workrooms, bathrooms, and closets was commonplace on the road. I stood by the sinks of a bathroom at New York's Lincoln Center, my breast pump plugged into an electric socket, while older ladies in fur coats washed their hands and gaped at my immodest setup. They would be even more shocked to see me onstage minutes later. My partner fended off our hungry children while I was delayed on subway platforms or at department meetings; the kids sucked on emptied bottles.

The World Health Organization and the American Academy of Pediatrics recommend differing amounts of time for exclusive breastfeeding, but so many of us mothers were not able to follow their guidelines. Some friends and their children weren't able to breastfeed, or chose not to; others didn't have the space and flexibility to continue after a short six-to-eight-week maternity leave from a high-pressure job, sometimes without pay.

My older child was nine months old and close to weaning herself completely, but travels to Italy and France for international string quartet competitions interfered with her plans; on the road she demanded to nurse five or six times a day. I returned to middle-of-the-night feedings while performing in competition rounds during the day. My younger child traveled with me on every trip starting at six weeks old. In order to get them an infant passport photo for a trip to Germany, I had to tilt their tiny head up towards the camera; their chin barely skimmed the photo. They were still nursing on their first birthday, and at thirteen months I decided I would not bring them down to Corpus for a repeat visit.

——— ᵔᴐ

Body and weakness; healing and strength. Looking out over the crowd, I introduce the final piece, the last movement of Johannes Brahms's string quartet in A minor. Thanks to press coverage, a full audience of varied ages and backgrounds is here from all over Corpus. The House of Rock regulars want to check us out and have a beer. Chamber music fans have showed up in excitement to hear us for a third visit in Corpus, this time in a bar, a first attempt at partnership between the Corpus Christi Chamber Music Society and House of Rock. I tell the packed room that we will share a drink with them afterwards.

We launch into the music, swaying together with energy and poise. Right before the end, at the music's low point, the audience is the quietest they have been all night. With a slight rise of my eyebrows I cue the others and we tear into the blistering ending. Over in a minute, it is the fastest and wildest we have played it. A man wearing Harley Davidson clothing from head to toe claps louder than anyone else. A few students cheer.

This performance marked the end of a year involving real physical worry for me: an injury in my left hand, stemming from stress and anxiety, had affected my ability to play. Dipping low for many months, I wondered if I would be able to keep concertizing. Recently I had been cautious onstage, holding back emotionally to monitor my playing health. But that evening in Corpus, I had no concern. I felt somatically cohesive for the first time in a year.

Close to midnight I walked back to my hotel in the humid air. The atmosphere inside of the bar was festive, but outside, Corpus felt serene. From my hotel room window the lights of the swimming pool ten floors below sparkled in the chlorinated blue. United States, Texan, and Mexican flags rustled out front in the light wind while the ocean appeared unmoving in the distance.

In this glow I pondered whether or not Corpus Christi is a dreamlike land where our defenses are laid bare and our bodies can find peace and solace, or if it is just another instance of Texan coastal sprawl. Perhaps the factory city marks a boundary between common life and the truer, better reality, a place on the sea where we can become somatically whole.

In 1916, historian Mary A. Sutherland describes, "Corpus Christi, quiet, queenly and beautiful, she lies on the warm white sands, like a mermaid taking a rest after her bath in the sparkling waters at her feet." As we cross the bridge into this "queenly" city maybe we are protected from harm and insult.

But remembering those ugly plumes of smoke I knew this was mostly wishful thinking. Strangely, I found myself in the pseudo-island community of Corpus Christi at key stages of my memory and development: a young artist, a new mother, a woman leaping into her professional life, an artist at a high career point. Nervous, tired, milk-smeared, injured, uplifted—my body holds the well-earned memories of four South Texan welcomes.

notes for themselves

PROTEST AND COMMUNITY

(for my children: shapeshifters, creators, persons outside the binary)

One child identifies as non-binary. One child identifies as cisgender female. One child carries a collar chain with "they-them" pronoun pins in their pocket to an event; they check to see who is there before pinning the words carefully to each side of their shirt collar. One child adjusts the computer camera so that school peers can see the wall-sized rainbow flag in the room. One child tells me that gender is over. One child collects stares from the older ladies in our neighborhood who don't know how to categorize them; the ladies' eyes narrow as we walk to catch the 1 train. One child is exasperated by societal pressure to remove body hair; she wears short shorts and smiles when others gaze at her visible leg hair. One child trembles after a session with a mentor who had trouble hearing about their pronouns; they shut the door to their room, put on their headphones, and listen to loud music until dinner.

Both children claim the colors of many LGBTQIA+ flags: purple, yellow, white, black, green, pink. We hold hands when walking by judgmental faces; march for love and human rights; address those who don't realize they are being offensive. The impulse to protect my children from harm is strong, but I know they don't need my physical support. They regularly demonstrate their power and wisdom.

At the 2017 Women's March in Lincoln, Nebraska, we held up our signs, we cheered. Even dogs wore T-shirts. We stood with those we didn't know previously and chanted, "This is what democracy looks like!" As we marched to the state capitol building looming over the prairie, we passed the Phi Gamma Delta fraternity at the University of Nebraska-Lincoln. About twenty-five young men sneered from their balcony and taunted us, "Build that wall!" They flew their blue and white Trump flags.

Holding my violin and standing with my older child and other string players in Washington Square Park at a 2020 vigil for Elijah McClain, a Black violinist murdered by the police, I tried to find musicians I knew. Most of the other people looked to be in their 20s. We gathered in a large group in front of the Arch holding our instruments, all masked, all ready. A few people had taped sheet music to their backs—"We Shall Overcome" and "Lift Every Voice." We also improvised—leaders ran through the group, calling out "B minor" or "A Major" to signify the key of the upcoming song. A community orchestra of violin, viola, cello, and bass voices lifted music up into the late June night sky.

After protests I scroll through websites trying to track the numbers in different cities. The data is sometimes hard to parse, and it's inexact across reporting. Did 500,000 people march in the Women's March on Washington, and 2.9 million nationwide; or 1 million people in Washington, and 4.5 million people worldwide? CBS said there were 200,000 people at the March for Our Lives in D.C. while organizers said 800,000. How many hundreds of people met at Stonewall for the July 2020 Black Trans Lives Matter rally? Will the numbers show proof of a united uprising?

Community and *communicate* come from the same French root, *commun,* meaning "common." Bryan Stevenson, an activist and lawyer for people on death row, writes, "our brokenness is the source of our common humanity, the basis for our shared search for comfort, meaning, and healing." By admitting and sharing our mistakes and vulnerabilities, we move a little closer towards each other. When injustice after injustice create a pattern of improbable normalcy, we become immune and tired. Tight bonds enable our survival.

In Cincinnati, Ohio
El Paso, Texas
Laramie, Wyoming
Biddeford, Maine
Cochiti Pueblo, New Mexico
Flint, Michigan
Galveston, Texas
Monroeville, Alabama
Lewiston, Idaho
Orlando, Florida
Honolulu, Hawaii

there is community. And people with whom to share indignation, love, triumph, and our common brokenness. The circle keeps widening.

I stand with my children. When we breathe together, our shared understanding multiplies. They continue to answer my questions about gender and sexuality with kind, measured voices, including me in their communities. But these are not my stories—I cannot decide where or if they begin or end. Their stories are like water meandering through its various forms and shapes and names, still retaining its essential qualities: vibrancy, fluidity, sparkle. All waters eventually flow into one.

becoming a more
resonant body

Perhaps it's stress, waiting backstage in the dark theater without being able to play or vocalize, but I am unnecessarily cold. I can see that the lights onstage are warm, even hot. My throat feels like wood dust. I take one or two sips of water and pace around in my heels, feeling as tall as possible. I adjust my jumpsuit, fixing the way it falls over the silver toes of my boots. The woman speaking to the audience has been plugging the next concert in the series— isn't it wonderful that the vocal octet will be back again! She walks offstage to mild applause and gives me a smile and a wink—you're on. I take a large breath, pull myself up again to my full height, and walk beyond the ridge of curtains into the bright lights.

While I make my way to the center of the stage I hear clapping. The lights obscure the audience from my view. I bow. A hoot from a friend gets swallowed easily in the dark theater. Then I am alone with a violin. No music stand, nothing else onstage. In my head I hear the first notes I will play as I raise my violin to my shoulder. Words, what are the words!? Panic settles in for a moment, but I pinpoint the text that I need.

My soul said to me: "I am sick."

I have rehearsed the emotional journey of this piece many times. The subject of my performance is a young woman questioning her life purpose while the world crumbles around her. My legs, unstable backstage, are now strong. I start the violin introduction—the beautiful familiarity of playing my instrument calms me. Thirty seconds into the piece another deep, clear voice rises over the violin:

I answered: "And I am sick."
"We may be well," said my soul. "Why are we not well?"
"How may we be well?" I asked.

These voices are both independent, sometimes at odds, intertwining in unexpected ways. Both are mine. My body heats up quickly as I move and bend with the music, as I sing and play. I engage all of myself. There can be nothing to hide.

"We may throw away all our vanity and false pride,"
said my soul. "We may take on a new life."

Finding one's voice suggests a journey, a progression through time, the goal of which is to become self-aware and assertive. Theoretically we can continually search for our voices, but cultural convention seems to suggest that there is a moment when our true voice is "found," when we come into ourselves. Maybe we decide on a vocation, or we rise to a place of unselfconsciousness in our life.

For a singer, the journey to find their voice is both a discovery of sound as well as a personal awakening, a deepening. In the German system of assigning a voice type, called a *Fach,* certain types take many years, sometimes into a singer's 40s, to reach a settled place. Although not every voice can be easily categorized using the *Fach* system, a woman who thought she was a mezzo-soprano could be surprised to learn in her late 30s that her voice type has stabilized into that of a dramatic soprano. Suddenly formidable operatic roles like Turandot in Giacomo Puccini's *Turandot,* Elsa in Richard Wagner's *Lohengrin,* or Marie in Alban Berg's *Wozzeck* might work best for her vocal range.

> "We may learn to wait and to possess ourselves
> in patience. We may labor and overcome."

In Willa Cather's novel *The Song of the Lark,* the main character Thea Kronborg struggles to identify as an artist after growing up in a rural Colorado community mostly unfamiliar with the world of serious musical study. Taking money left to her by a late suitor, she travels to Chicago to pursue the piano and later discovers that she wants to develop her singing voice. She turns her ambition to becoming a singer, in future years inhabiting colossal Wagnerian operatic roles in Europe. Kronberg knows how she will contribute artistically to the world once she claims her voice. As Cather writes: "Artistic growth is, more than it is anything else, a refining of the sense of truthfulness."

This sense of truthfulness is a kind of test of the soul. An artist may practice all day—honing their instrumental or vocal skills, dancing with grace, sculpting stone—and their consistency and dedication may be noble. However, their ego still questions the value of the art they create and the quality of their talent, including their ability to execute their task. This is a battle between the artistic ego and artistic freedom, a fight that threatens to block the road towards self-discovery. Self-examination moves an artist's journey forward as well as hinders it. Nothing involving the growth of expression moves in a straight line.

> "We can do none of these things," I cried. "Have I
> not tried all of them some time in my short life?"

Resonance, as defined by the *Oxford English Dictionary,* is "the expression of energy, transferred through a material which can hold the energy." I coax resonance out of the wooden chamber of my violin, and when I play, my body helps to carry the violin's resonance. Any tension in my body while playing inhibits my ability to carry the sound's full vibrations. In a much more direct way, a singer's very insides—bones, water, organs—function as a resonance chamber for their sound to enter the world. Through study and experience a voice resonates exponentially larger.

> "And have I not waited and wanted until you have
> become faint with pain? Have I not looked and longed?"

In 2013 I decided to perform a series of works for a singing violinist—violin and voice, performed by one person—written by composer Lisa Bielawa. My sister Abigail, a singer, introduced me to Bielawa's *Kafka Songs,* which use haunting texts from Franz Kafka's *Meditations.* I found the idea of singing and playing together both terrifying and thrilling. It's the rubbing-head-patting-stomach routine, but times fifty, especially when the music is rhythmically and textually complex. At first when attempting to read two lines of music at the same time, one the violin line and the other the vocal part, I was overwhelmed. Singing in tune with my instrumental playing was especially difficult. I separated one musical part from the other, one measure at a time, slowly realizing that performing in this way might be possible. Still, my small but clear voice could barely sing over the sound of my violin. How could I trust my resonance to grow?

"Dear soul, why do you not resign yourself? Why can you not stay quiet and trouble yourself and me no more?"

In three voice lessons, my sister challenged me to draw my strength from the earth. I found a deeper vocal tone by bending my knees and attempting to lift the piano, putting my hands underneath the keyboard. She also stressed the importance of having a character motivation for every word and phrase I sang. It occurred to me that although it's never a worthwhile goal, a violinist can sometimes "get away" with a mildly boring performance, the aim of which is technical, like good intonation or clarity of bow strokes. But when words are involved, their meaning has to be the focus—vocal performances disengaged from the text are automatically flat and worthless.

Owning my voice was the hardest part of the process. Even though I practiced the vocal part extensively, I had trouble knowing how I sounded. Part of this was situational. I can trust the sound coming out of my violin because the instrument is close to my ear, but a singer can never fully "hear" their sound. They must count on recordings and other people's ears to know what is being conveyed to the audience.

From a psychological perspective, it was easy to make excuses for my voice—I'm not *really* a singer, but I'm doing these pieces

. . . I'm primarily a violinist, really *only* a violinist, etc.—but that attitude prevented me from committing to my sound, however small or wobbly it seemed at the moment. Perhaps if I found peace with my voice, I would find it resembled my more assured violin playing.

> "Why are you always straining and reaching? There
> isn't anything for you. You are wearing yourself out."

Three years after my first foray into singing and playing, I was both eager and anxious to sing a piece written for me by Bielawa, *One Atom of Faith.* A work of remarkable urgency and intimacy, the passionate text is by Mary MacLane, an early-20th century American autobiographical writer. MacLane is a nineteen-year-old confronting her existence and wondering how she can extricate herself from the malaise of self-questioning. The young woman and her soul, presented as two separate entities, converse with one another, seeking relief from the sense of being unwell. The back and forth creates an ideal opportunity for the voice and the violin to act as side-by-side characters in dramatic dialogue. Bielawa assigns the violin to play one part and the voice to sing the other. The conflict between the two temperaments results in the young woman having greater resolve. She declares at the end of the work, "I will keep one atom of faith in love, in truth, and the truth that is love."

Even though I had been living with Bielawa's mesmerizing music for several years, I still felt inadequate as a singing violinist. Was I waiting for permission? Was I merely posing as a vocalist? The excuses I gave others about how I was not really a singer held me back. When I finally sang *One Atom of Faith* for the composer, she looked at me intensely and said, "I did not write this for a trained operatic singer. I wrote it for you. You can stop worrying about trying to achieve a perfect vocal technique. That's not the point. Be who you are, but also be the 19-year-old woman who is alone and afraid of her awesome power. Be *her*."

"My soul made answer: 'I may strain and reach
until only one worn nerve of me is left.'"

After the composer's galvanizing comments, I memorized the music to fully internalize it. I imagined how the writer might feel in 1901, as a young woman in Montana with artistic dreams and no one to make sense of her work. I envisioned her lonely sobbing late at night. The more that I embodied the writer's predicament the less careful my singing sounded. Sometimes I whispered, sometimes I cried, and sometimes I spoke when the vocal pitches were low. When I heard recordings of myself, I was surprised by the force of my sound. My voice lost its hesitation when I was pushed to the edge of expression. Similar to the struggle and reconciliation in MacLane's text, a transformation was happening inside of me—I let myself embody a wider sort of resonance. *One Atom of Faith* was forcing me to find an emotional threshold, which in turn constituted finding part of my voice. My violin and my voice started sounding, together, unrestrained.

"And that one nerve may be scourged
with whips and burned with fire.
But I will keep one atom of faith."

As I broaden my artistic practice into writing songs for myself to perform, the creative act requires a wild, almost mad sensibility. It's not about finding a *Fach* or wielding perfection. It's about gaining an expressive edge that might not be growing *into* one's voice, but instead finding other compartments in one's body, or even finding one's body elsewhere. Singer Tom Waits said of his songwriting, "You put yourself into some kind of trance to receive certain songs." How can we expand the idea of a resonant body, and where it can be activated? Which resonant bodies will emerge in our next decades, and how can we be ready to hear them?

"I may go bad, but I will keep one atom of
faith in Love and in the Truth that is Love.
I will keep one atom of faith."

—Mary MacLane, 19 years old, Butte, Montana, 1901

in the air

The Delta Airbus overhead looks like a toy being pulled across the sky—its compact white shape with recognizable red and blue tail could have been painted by an artist specializing in miniatures. It must be too small to fit real humans. The jet leaves my window view, the white now reflecting pink in the setting sun. The westward-facing buildings gather crimson light at their edges, framing the beginning of evening. I have to close my eyes to remember the adrenaline of flight, the push and pull of lift, how g-force affects my body.

———

Tonight I sit in my orange-and-white-striped chair by the window for over an hour, and in this time only twenty-two people come out of the subway station. Nine enter. I see one person wearing blue scrubs. At 7:30 p.m. six months ago, the A train station entrance was packed with bodies dressed in suits, skirts, and hoodies, carrying bags and briefcases, shuttling children in strollers. The shadows lengthen. 7 p.m. used to be the hour to clap, cheer, and

37

bang pots for the health-care workers. Every night I yelled until I was hoarse—my voice never sounded loud enough.

———⁓

Before the pandemic, some of us followed Greta Thunberg's daring Atlantic voyage from the UK to New York on a zero-carbon emission yacht. I noticed other public figures giving online instead of in-person interviews to raise climate change awareness. But almost no one (except Thunberg's mother, a musician) was willing to give up a thriving career to reduce their carbon footprint. There was not yet enough pressure to make real, global sacrifice. Only the bravest asked: what would our lives be like without air travel?

I wonder, with no regret or sadness, if I will ever fly again.

———⁓

"Hi," I greeted two TWA flight attendants on my way off the plane, my entire body one highly taut muscle. "I'm wondering if I could ask both of you something: that was really bad, right? I mean, I have never seen so many belongings staying up in the air as we fell, so many times."

"Yes, you're right," said the tall, slender attendant, pushing her long, straight brown hair out of her face, revealing a wrinkled brow. "It was probably the worst flight I've been on in fifteen years of working in the airline industry."

The shorter attendant, a woman with dark curly hair and red lipstick, shook her head. "Terrible."

I passed the cockpit and said with mock cheerfulness, "Thanks for saving our lives" to the blond-haired pilot who looked young enough to be my age, right out of graduate school. He turned around and grinned. "We deal with what Mother Nature gives us."

———✦———

I experienced too many near-misses—accidents, severe storms, eternally long drops—to ever feel completely secure in the air. I was physically safe but felt psychologically damaged by the anxiety. I dreamt nightly of falling off of buildings in the clouds, of plummeting in elevators riding up to the sky on thin wires. My fear seemed impossible to overcome.

———✦———

1. Avoidance: first, refusing to fly on a few flights; driving many hours to my destination instead.
2. Obsessive, insatiable research: reading books on weather systems; speaking to pilots on and off the ground; pouring over turbulence reports; watching flight simulations on the Hurricane Hunters website and biting the inside of my cheeks as they flew through the storms' eyewalls. How bad could it get? Had I experienced the worst?
3. Counting: similar to measuring my strokes in the pool swimming long distances, I counted during turbulence at a tempo of 60 beats per minute. This was productive. I could also test my musician's perfect tick—could I keep up a pace of exactly 60? The pilot announced it would be bumpy for twenty minutes, so I would close my eyes and start: 1 . . . 33, 34 . . . 59, 60, 1, 2 . . . repeat. Twenty minutes is either long or short depending on your viewpoint, but the beat stays the same.

———✦———

In a way, I was happiest on flights when traveling with babies—taking care of someone gave me purpose. My children were my flight companions when they were young. The smaller the human the more stuff that human needs, so I dragged Pack 'n Plays, strollers, and car seats across the US and Europe in order that my tiny humans could be with me.

———

The flight attendant heard fussing and came over to us. "Oh, little sweetheart, look at that sad face! Don't worry, we'll be landing soon and you won't have all that pressure on your ears!"

Suddenly my infant child stopped crying and looked up in the direction of the attendant, but past her, with wet eyes bright and open. She widened her petite lips into a radiant, unearthly smile.

"Now *that* is special: your baby is seeing an angel."

———

When I was alone on the plane, my fixated counting practice evolved into a kind of memorization. The sequential repetition of numbers led to musical sounds and phrases playing over and over in my head. Staring at the white cloud beds below, bumping through the air, the music often sounded clearer than it did on the ground. The time could become a valuable commodity, a present.

———

Even so, I was always aware of the cost to myself and the people I left. Alone in hotels around the world, I longed to hold a small, soft hand, to hum a loved one to sleep.

———

They were mad when I came home. They hid their feelings behind celebratory pasta dinners and chewy homemade cookies and wanting me to scratch their backs before bed. But their lives had changed without my participation. I was afraid every time that I had been gone too long.

———~⌒

"Mom, how many days?"

"I leave early tomorrow and then I'll be back in four days, on Monday, not a long trip."

"Ok . . . but, Mom?"

"Yes?"

"When is this going to end, again? Like, when will you be home for good?"

———~⌒

Complaining, testing, trying to prove how much I cared about everyone—I was a mess before any trip. Once, I spent money we didn't have on a large children's kitchen set, which I assembled ferociously before I left. Another time I was up until my alarm at 3:30 a.m. gluing a diorama assignment. Would my four-year-old really remember a board tacked with twelve envelopes, one to open for each day I was gone? Did I do this just to ease my fear of being forgotten, of becoming invisible?

———~⌒

Professional travelers aim for invisibility and anonymity. They wait in their impeccable suits and Tumi luggage in front of the First Class or Premium signs. They don't mix with the civilians on vacation, sporting flip-flops in the winter and drinking "red beer" (light beer with Bloody Mary mix and green olives) at 7:00 a.m. at the bar. The infrequent travelers ask too many questions at the security line; they have trouble removing their shoes and figuring out how to put their electronic devices into separate bins; they tie up long lines. The professionals, on the other hand, show their special badges, slip past the crowds, and melt into the fabric of the airport. They take up zero space. One never knows they are there.

———

They also take up as much space as they want, whenever they want.

"What is that, is that sheet music?" The heavy-set, doughy-elbowed man wearing a black T-shirt and shorts with white sneakers leaned over to me. Fortunately, since we were in the plane's first row, a large plastic barrier stood in between me and the man's rum-and-Coke breath.

"Yes," I said, briefly turning. "I'm studying." I put my head down again, closer to the page.

"Oh wow, a *real* musician! You know, I just came from Mar-a-Lago and I heard some good stuff down there at their club." He sighed peacefully. "That was a good time."

"Uh huh. Look, I hope you don't mind, but I'm working right now. I have a concert tonight."

"Okay, I'll wait until you're done. You know, I've been waiting the whole flight to talk to you." He slurped down his third drink.

———

Getting upgraded regularly to first class and eating at posh international lounges certainly held an appeal for a middle-class concert violinist. Having membership in the elite society of frequent travelers was like playing dress-up. It was a side life in which I could pretend I wasn't struggling to pay the bills in my real life. But at the core of that life for me were loneliness and disconnection.

———

For a while I convinced myself the views were worth it. I kept track of sunrises from the plane, saved multiple photos per week of saturated orange and purple skies blending into one another. The way a thin line of brilliance opens up as the misty dawn exchanges places with the wideness of day. Or the companionship of the stars and moon while flying to Europe under the cover of night, following the curve of Earth.

———

One March morning we descended into Copenhagen, coming out of the thick clouds to view a large wind farm in the North Sea. The gathering of identical silver blades cycling wildly in the wind looked like a new kind of survivalist landscape rising out of the ocean. I imagined the turbines to be sucking us out of the sky, drawing us to the earth. Each time we dipped in the wind I wondered if the sea would claim our tiny plane as an offering to an elemental spirit. Would we be a casualty of these eager machines, testing the limits of human power? Was our suffering planet calling us back home?

———

I get up from my striped chair and stretch out from sitting so long. Hearing murmurs from my children's room, I yawn and look at the time. We were obviously not meant to live in the sky—we have enough to do down here. The nighttime cityscape will soon begin to roll out its light show.

the living, breathing memory of wood

As I pause to examine the clay objects' textures, the work that went into their making becomes clearer to me. Each piece has a different size and shape, but two things connect them. One is their material: the rough reddish and brown clay appears unfinished, almost in-process, even though the pieces have already been fired in the kiln. The second is the empty space: somewhere in each object's body is a circular depression, showing that it has encountered, at least once, a rounded clay tool. Many of the objects can fit in one hand; others are the size of medium or large mixing bowls; a third group is thicker and elongated, like a row of flower planters that has been manipulated and distorted.

I try to imagine the objects' functions—are these clay pieces designed to hold liquid, fruit, or plants at odd angles? Some appear to defy function. I view their shapes and holes as evidence of motion. In an object's twist, for example, I know the maker's gesture. I can grasp the tool rolling through the clay. The artist tells us, "the work is finished when it represents what really happens in the action of doing it."

In December 2009 I waited in a packed line with other tourists, New Yorkers, and art aficionados to view Mexican artist Gabriel Orozco's retrospective at the Modern Museum of Art. Once in the galleries I was drawn immediately to a "multi-cycle" hanging from the ceiling. Its seven or eight wheels connected by the thin pipes used for bicycle construction defied physics, raising questions about how one might ride such a vehicle. Did Orozco build it just to challenge our worldview? Is it actually drivable, and by how many people? Another altered vehicle was parked on the ground: a French car made by Citroën that was half of its original size. From the side it looked like a normal, small car, but from the front I could see its shrunken width. Orozco had sliced the car down the middle and refashioned it such that only a small seat and the steering wheel remained inside.

Every piece in the show was conceptually ambitious and impressively made or reimagined, but the variety of the materials confused me. Orozco had made intricate drawings on airline boarding passes; he had tacked plastic tops of yogurt containers to the wall. I wondered if the work's disparate materials showed the artist's inability to focus. Was he afraid of going deep into the work? Maybe his lack of specialization in any one medium prevented me from glimpsing his vision.

I found out afterwards that Orozco is adamantly uninterested in becoming a specialist. In fact, his conceptual practice often celebrates the wonder and perspective of a beginner, a hobbyist. Not only does he refuse to keep a studio, he travels to locations to make work that reflects the character of the place, using site-specific materials. In a short film "Thinking with Clay," Orozco obtains hearty clay from a French ceramic workshop that was formerly a brick factory. He fashions crudely shaped vessels, some of which resemble pots. The point of this exercise is not to make perfectly sculpted ceramic objects; it is to see the process of creation in the thing that has been made.

While sitting on my apartment floor watching the artist work in the French brick factory, I realize that he and I share an interest in the energy of objects. I had been wrestling with his work and why a plastic top to a yogurt container belonged in a museum. But in thinking of a material's ability to effect animacy, I found an entry point into Orozco's vision. Perhaps he too is fascinated by imprints, the way an object and its user carry and leave traces. Could the yogurt tops, created for a utilitarian function, carry traces as well? Was questioning their past, current, and future purpose part of the artwork? I wonder what Orozco might instantly understand about my world of string instruments, as well as the energy found in wood.

———

Stringed instrument makers have been using wood for centuries because of its strength; if cared-for, wooden objects are able to stay intact for hundreds of years. Wood is also used for its breathability, its resonant and vibratory qualities. As evidenced by the rings seen in some trees, wood can hold lives and show the marking of time. When I read C. S. Lewis's *The Chronicles of Narnia* to my children, it had been years since I first thought about the books' magic wardrobe. A wardrobe made out of the tree becomes a portal into Narnia, the world from where the tree came. The transition of a magical tree to its product now seemed more poignant after spending years as a professional violinist.

While the world of string playing makes no claims to magic, many musicians, including myself, believe that something akin to a spirit lies in each violin. Every time I have searched for a new violin I have known within a few minutes if it is "the one." There is a spark I have learned to trust, an excitement flowing through my body as my bow unites with the violin strings, a knowing. My violin may sound flat in another's hands even though it sings in mine. Not unlike the search for a life partner, players will look for years, even traveling around the world to find our wooden soul mates. The closeness with an instrument keeps our playing fresh and moving forward, and the frustration with an instrument can stagnate a career. We rely on an instrument to challenge and provoke us to develop further as artists.

When I first played my current violin, an instrument made in the early 1800s in Naples, Italy, I perceived a golden aura surrounding me. It was such a powerful sensation that I almost put the violin down in surprise. My previous violin had a deep and wise character, but it was not bright enough to convey sound to a large concert hall. I was looking for an instrument that could be heard well without being obnoxiously loud. While playing the Neapolitan violin, I felt I had met my match, but in unreal abundance—like seeing the positive qualities of a new love interest in hyper color after going through a difficult breakup. It was clear to me that this violin was the next step.

The personalities found in instruments are no accident—they are the combination of visionary craftsmanship and the right kinds of wood. Brazilian Pernambuco, for example, has been used for over 250 years to make violin bows. When wood supplies dwindled to dangerous lows due to deforestation crises in Brazil, makers started experimenting with synthetic materials like carbon fiber and fiberglass. I own two carbon fiber bows, quite well-crafted and easy to play, however the comparison to their wooden counterparts is stark. Synthetic bows feel light and springy in my right hand, and I can play them anywhere—outdoors, in schools with young children—without fear that they will be damaged. However, the way a Pernambuco bow bends delicately as I draw it across the strings, taking my intention, is a much more integrated experience. Because of the wood's pliability, bows can be continually reshaped through the delicacy of recambering, a process in which makers change the wood's density throughout the stick using a hot flame. It is its own kind of sorcery.

Similarly, violin, viola, cello, and bass makers scrutinize each piece of wood for the bodies of their instruments. They sometimes travel to a forest, as Orozco might do, to pick out the wood by hand. Makers, like players, also trust their instincts to know when a piece of wood is right for an instrument. They research the forests and the weather; they develop relationships with the people working with trees; they analyze the properties of the wood—thickness, density, grain. The maker of my friend's viola flew to Cremona, Italy, to select a piece of spruce for the top of his instrument. He already had a fine piece of maple for the instrument's back but needed to find its match. Upon his return, the maker and my friend spent hours together looking at pictures of the forest from where the wood was chosen, speaking about the character of the sound my friend loved and wanted in his viola. They held the wood in their hands, feeling a connection to the material. The viola possesses unique qualities because of the intention that went into its creation. Nothing mass-produced can initially communicate that same kind of touch and care.

The movie *The Red Violin* chronicles the tale of a seventeenth-century violin, the people who played on it, and the way it traveled throughout the centuries. Although this is a somewhat sensationalist account (spoiler alert: the red quality of the instrument's varnish is attributed to the maker's wife's blood added to the mix), the idea the film presents, of a magnificently crafted violin that has a distinctive personality and takes on the qualities of its players, is accurate. Some notable instruments have nicknames based on their past owners. The "Rose" Stradivarius cello (now played by Yo Yo Ma), for example, is so designated because the famous cellist Leonard Rose was the cello's owner for many years, and the way he played was indelibly marked into the cello's resonance chamber. While I have never known the complete histories of the instruments I have owned and played, I enjoy imagining what their past lives contained.

———⌁——

This particular violin had an urgency about it. It seemed to be crying out, to be left alone. Its owner's intensity was apparent after only a few notes—I could feel her desire to push every inch of this violin's sound out. I was alternating between playing an instrument my friend had owned for ten years, and the violin she was thinking about buying. She sat in front of me, her face intent with listening as I played a solo work by J. S. Bach and a violin concerto by Béla Bartók on both instruments. No matter what music I played, the impression of her violin stayed the same: my friend had wrung out every last bit of this violin's resonance. Her frustration at her violin's inability to do what she wanted as a musician had become tangible, captured in her violin's resonance chamber.

After this experience I started to see if I could "hear" a previous owner in other violins I tried. It was often hard to tell if an instrument's reluctance to speak or inability to be quiet was a quality of its own—"this violin is an introvert," for example, or "this violin cannot make a pale color; it sounds loud even when played gently." I discovered that sometimes my initial impressions were off. What seemed like a shy instrument, for example, could open up quickly when I used a more forceful approach. A violin that was played for many years by an aggressive person expected robust treatment, but it could get used to a calmer touch. Most instruments sitting unplayed in a shop, a museum, or a collector's home respond awkwardly when first played; they are temperamental as they are being awakened. Musicians need time playing an unused instrument to get its resonance spinning once again. In this way, becoming acquainted with an instrument is its own kind of sculpting.

Many Stradivari violins, with and without nicknames, are legendary for the variety of color in their sounds but also for their unruliness. A mentor of mine compared performing on a celebrated Strad, an instrument we had both played, to "trying to tame a wild stallion." Over many years the violin had taken on its own ego and complexity, almost a defensive posture; it seemed to challenge those who thought they could make it sound beautiful. Perhaps this personality was in the violin's nature from the beginning, and possibly also in the maker's intention, but it could have been the result of many strong players battling it throughout the centuries. If a player released their need for ownership, the violin exploded with color and depth and brilliance. Conversely, if a player didn't let go of their own needs, the violin rebelled by sounding tight, dry, and unable to manage. Thus, the concept that great instruments "play themselves."

When playing a violin like a Strad or Guarneri for short periods of time I have learned to let the instrument lead me. I need to hear, not just imagine, its secrets. Only then can we leave imprints on each other.

"I love the way you've fixed this up," I said, looking around my grandmother's new living room. I was sipping whiskey out of a shot glass. It was 10:30 p.m., late for my grandmother, but she had insisted on my visiting her right after flying in from New York. Her new home was down the street from my parents' place in Houston, Texas, small and ideal for one person, including a garage apartment that she rented out to music students from Rice University.

"You can never tell what's going on up there," my grandmother said of the young woman renting the apartment. "I wish she would throw a party or something, get out once in a while. She's such a bore."

My grandmother's thin, dyed-brown, shoulder-length hair was set off haphazardly to the right side of her face with a golden clip, and she was wearing a set of bright jewelry from one of her many adventures: a gold bracelet, necklace, and earrings with matching orange stones that sparkled in the lamp light. I admired her distinctive taste and non-apologetic manner. Even in the way she set up her home—we sat on a birch couch with white cushions looking at pieces of Chinese, Taiwanese, and African art purchased from artists she knew—one could tell that this woman cared about appearance. She also desired to shock and provoke in her sly way.

"Grandma," I said. "Are you having friends over these days?"

"Who needs them," she said, laughing. "So many of them are almost dead anyways, but I suppose I keep a few. It's good to have some. When your parents invite me over I won't feel like I'm such a hanger-on."

She took a sip from the whiskey in her hand and put it down on the rim of her wooden bar. The size of a rolltop desk and made of teak wood, this bar was a prominent feature of her living room.

I could see the red and blue lights from the furniture store across the street reflecting in the mirrors as the large doors sat open, welcoming.

The smell and the look of the teak bar with its aged wood, mirrors, and old-fashioned (and Old Fashioned) tumblers made of thick, diamond-detailed glass, were relics of my early life. I had never opened the bar doors by myself, but I did peer in while they were open, seeing my curious, child's eyes in the mirrors running along the backside, my reflection interrupted by bottles of Irish whiskey and vodka. Bourbon and cherry juice had become embedded in the wood over many decades; the scent was sweet and melancholic.

I associated the bar with my serious and brilliant grandfather, a scholar whose presence evoked reverence and a little fear. I knew not to disturb him in the early mornings while he read the *New York Times,* worked on the crossword puzzle, and drank coffee. Once leaving the foreign service, he retreated into a life of hermetic scholarship and teaching; not many people came over to my grandparents' house at the end of his life. Even when we visited my grandmother in Houston after my grandfather died, the bar commanded a magisterial presence, its fragrance permeating the room although my grandmother hadn't made an Old Fashioned in years.

As if in response to my thoughts, my grandmother reached for her glass and held it up high in the air, "When I croak, you guys get the bar."

Sometimes my grandmother could make arbitrary statements, but this sounded like an official announcement.

"Grandma . . . are you sure?" I asked.

"Don't be silly. Toast to a fleeting life," she said with a dramatic flourish, and downed her drink.

My grandmother was in her 80s at that time and in excellent health despite her life-long smoking habit. She would remain the employed organist at a Methodist church up until the age of ninety, after which she passed away peacefully. Only months prior to her death, she had played her final church service with customary zeal (even though she had almost completely lost her hearing). Weeks later, my parents sent movers to pack up the bar and ship it to our home.

My first memories of the bar date back to the 1980s, when my mother's parents lived in Lawrenceville, New Jersey. We would drive five-and-a-half hours from southern Vermont, and once we started covering our noses from New Jersey's factory emissions, I knew we were close to our destination. We parked in front of my grandparents' modest, ranch-style brick house, and my sister and I ran up the front steps to the sound of the barking poodle, Guifei. (The dog was named for Yang Guifei, a consort of emperor Xuanzong of the Tang dynasty—my grandfather was teaching ancient Chinese military history at the time). My grandfather greeted us at the front door holding an Old Fashioned cocktail for each of my parents. The kids were served Shirley Temples.

He had mixed all of the drinks in the bar, commissioned and made in Hong Kong in the 1950s when he was stationed there as a foreign diplomat. My mother and uncle learned later that he was working for the Central Intelligence Agency. Traveling by boat to each new location in the 1950s and 60s, my grandparents brought their bar with them for entertaining and for comfort. It was the only piece of furniture they commissioned, but it was also an instant excuse for a party. Contrary to media portrayals, diplomats are not often wealthy people, but they do move in the elite world of politicians and celebrities, and they host their own events from time to time. My grandparents certainly knew how to entertain. Singing and playing the piano, they took turns serving drinks to friends.

The bar was delivered to our home in 2009, a month, coincidentally, before we attended Gabriel Orozco's show at the MoMA. We spent almost an hour removing the heavy plastic wrapping surrounding the wood. Once we carefully opened the handmade compartment doors, the bar's unmistakable aroma came roaring out, startling me with memories of twenty-to-thirty years before. The bar lent a sense of legitimacy to our Nebraska dining room. In its look and smell one could see it had lived, that it deserved respect. One late winter's evening full of sleet and weather warnings, we invited friends to share drinks with us in honor of the bar's arrival, serving Old Fashioned and Negroni cocktails in pitchers from the bar. It seemed the most fitting way to celebrate the piece of furniture that had defined my grandparents' entertaining life for decades.

After the party we sat around our dining room table trying to piece together what we knew of the bar's experiences and travels, as we would of any person's life journey, or a violin's, for that matter. The bar was made in Hong Kong, crossed oceans by boat to Kenya and Pakistan and the States, then moved by truck to multiple US locations when my grandfather left the foreign service; it absorbed many conversations in European, African, and Asian languages; it most likely heard confidential government deliberations; it witnessed over-the-top performances of musical theater and hours of piano practice and improvisation. The wood, as a porous material, had gathered these experiences in its body, even if they were not expressed in any obvious way. We considered what our nuclear family might offer to the bar's list of activities for another generation or two: listening to hours of violin, viola, and flute practicing; attending poetry readings and theoretical and political discussions; surviving moves from Houston to Nebraska, then on to New York.

I was both in awe of the bar's life experience as well as frustrated that it was not able to communicate with me. I held the youthful hope that through the years its energy would be made apparent, in the way a violin's resonant chamber developed over time. But I knew that I was envisioning the impossible. Merely looking at or holding a violin would not make it come to life—it required being played to deepen and mature. Could I be content with the bar's practical function and the exceptional story of its past, without expecting it to take on a magical persona?

———

Working the lemon-scented oil into the wood felt like rubbing a child's back or brushing a dear pet's fur. It was an act of nurture, the only time I had been so close to a piece of wood besides my violin. The liquor area was stained with congealed cherry juice and spilled whiskey and bourbon, so I started my cleaning of the wood there. Wiping down all of the inner cabinets and their walls, then polishing the mirrors, was a rite of passage: the bar had declared us worthy of carrying it to its next chapter.

I ran the cloth along the outside of the bar, inspecting a large diagonal crack on one door to see how vulnerable it had become. We would need to repair it. After rubbing down the top of the bar I stood back to survey the lustrous wood, still moist from the oil. For a moment I feared that the cleaning may have dampened the bar's formidable smell, but upon opening the doors the bar's sensuous aroma flooded out.

In taking care of this well-traveled object in a new way, perhaps my actions were creating the connection I desired; perhaps the bar's energy was brought forth in a demand for excellent treatment. Would intention develop in an object merely from years of being used, a "realness" of imprint not imagined by its maker?

I left the doors open for the afternoon, secretly wishing the bar would engage in a process of taking root in its new environment when I wasn't looking. I had validated its arrival—how might it now adjust? Would the planks of the century-old wooden floor affix themselves to their new tenant's feet? Like the underground social connections found in forests, could the products of once-living trees bind together to create new ecosystems? The shadows of dusk descended, and the bar disappeared into night.

notes for themselves

SLEEP

(for my children: shapeshifters, creators, persons outside the binary)

Sleep is a guise you put on. Can anyone really tell if you've been engaged in it? What are the signs—sagging under the eyes, a dazed or pinched look, a slowness to respond. Its scarcity could appear in other ways—a jovial, over-caffeinated appearance, quick, harried eyes, a fine rise to anger. If you strive to appear functional, no one will know you are in want. Sleep is a kind of privilege because those who don't struggle don't know the gift of seven or eight hours. Our sleeping habits define us.

I was told I slept beautifully as a child, so I guess once it was up to me I messed up my sleeping gift. Then it was a choice, and there was always something better to do. I took walks in the middle of the night, sometimes alone, sometimes with friends, usually restless. A few times we met in a graveyard at 3:00 a.m. or snuck inside to listen to Zeppelin and Hendrix on vinyl. We felt rebellious at the time (sleep was available, though shunned), but all we did was walk between the moss-covered tombstones, yelling to the empty sky.

Initially, staying up late was imperative for me after days of being with so many people. The energy relaxed at night, and I could recharge. I painted, read, and listened—thoughts were uninterrupted. But night owl practices led me to the false belief that sleep was not always necessary. I could make it through, pushing without caffeine. Serious anxiety descended and later insomnia. Some nights I didn't even sleep fifteen minutes (sleep was now no longer a choice). Each day was its own survival. I searched for the shape of myself somewhere within the haze.

> My repertoire of sleep aids—
> melatonin and warm showers
> Ayurvedic oil massage
> yin yoga poses
> cherries at lunchtime
> one beer
> two beers
> no beers
> working out early
> working out close to bed.

One night trying sleeping pills felt like an artificial curtain muffling my consciousness. I fought the drug all night, decided it wasn't worth it. I would rather be in my head and face the monster.

I observed the low-worry people on planes and in cars. The plane was still at the gate and they snored away, heads gently bobbing with breath and the vehicle's humming. I held bitterness towards these people (so blissfully unaware of their gift). For just one twenty-four-hour period could they experience sleeplessness so that they could empathize? If I showed up for the day, awake since 1:45 a.m., my heart pounding too hard from exhaustion, they yawned and smiled with the crust of sleep still in the corners of their eyes. Or they expressed a not-hidden disdain in their raised eyebrows—"What is so wrong with you that you can't sleep night after night?" They took for granted my foremost desire.

If sleep is a basic human need, why does it feel like a luxury? The very concept of rest is forced to do battle with the hurried pace of our lives. In North America, the average amount of sleep for adults has decreased from ten hours in the early 20th century to six-and-a-half hours per night now. A "scandal of sleep," according to writer and art historian Jonathan Crary. In an age when progress has beaten out all else in the race for our time, sleep is not so much restorative but an activity we measure by how little we can get in order to survive.

Viewing sleep as a scandal is strangely comforting to me. The effort to obtain more than the several hours of tossing in bed is a fight shared amongst many. But is it 24/7 industry that keeps me from sleeping? Am I responding intuitively to a world gone increasingly haywire while it ignores the elements? At my most pathetic— martyr, victim—I imagine I am alone, battling an inner world. I am not a slave to my alarm or repressing my sleep for work, I just can't get there.

My adult life has been spent searching for sleep's specific value, questioning others' devotion to it, and reasserting new commitments to recuperative nights (and how much more appealing is rest when framed as a protest against 24/7 capitalism?!). Could we all learn to respond more closely to the planetary sequences of light and darkness, listening to the rhythm of a world in balance even if we, personally, are not? Perhaps then sleep would not have classes, the haves and have-nots. It would be yet again something that, as in earlier stages of the human race, was not seen as controversial.

Many humans struggle to rest. In Mumbai, Helsinki, Nairobi, Beijing, Atlanta—they sit at the bedsides of loved ones, get lost inside their heads, move under the cover of darkness. But is this sleepless state a gift, as well? Despite the malaise of insomnia and worry, sleeplessness does not always go unrewarded, especially as a planned activity. What if sleep is willingly sacrificed, for late nights and early mornings spent wishing, working, loving?

I have learned some secrets, not sleeping. When the hurt is greatest, when the inability to rest is genuine, guidance is also present. Sleepless ones take our turns gazing at the night sky, if we are able. Because the stars connect us everywhere, these constant, cold companions. We are reminded that other gifts—wide-awake dreaming, identifying the source of troubles, detecting solutions, baring vulnerabilities—lie within reach.

memorization and
the risk of nostalgia

Chris Marker's 1962 sci-fi film *La Jeteé* is set in a society that seeks nostalgics. While humans live underground and there are no options left for survival, certain men are subjected to medical experiments with the aim of going backwards or forwards in time to obtain food and to save the human race. Almost all of the subjects die or go mad. Only one man, selected for his "very strong mental images," is able to endure passage into the past. After an agonizing transition between time and space, he lives for a few months as an adult in a previous life. The depth of his nostalgia makes him an ideal candidate for these trials, and his accurate recall of childhood imagery enables his persistence through the time barrier.

In Marker's dystopian world the nostalgic's skills are prized and useful. However, the systematic recall he must perform in order to situate himself precisely in both his past and future lives causes him tremendous pain. His nostalgia is almost used as a weapon. As one prone to episodes of nostalgia myself, *La Jeteé* is empathetically excruciating for me to watch.

Even the mention of nostalgia can polarize a conversation quickly. Humans spend (and waste, depending on your viewpoint) ridiculous amounts of money and time trying to live in the past, through reconnecting with the music and materials of our old selves—think: conferences for adults who trade G. I. Joe figurines; businesses devoted to 80s dance party paraphernalia. Sometimes we refuse to move on from habits and resolutions we made at critical moments in our younger lives. The resistance to change is a powerful force, and nostalgia can be the indulgence we crave in vulnerable moments.

Nostalgia, whose Greek roots include *nostos*—the return home, and *algia*—longing, was treated in earlier times as a crushing medical condition from which soldiers were known to have died. It was literally "homesickness," a mental depression that brought on deterioration of the physical body. Longing for a home, time, or place that used to exist or perhaps never existed can engender unhealthy idolatry in addition to nostalgia's potentially catastrophic physical effects. It muddies a person's judgment and ability to see what is right in front of them. I can long for my hometown in Vermont and what I recall was an idyllic childhood there, but my fond memories may greatly obscure any difficulties inherent in my upbringing. Unrealistic longing in individuals and societies can have deleterious effects on entire generations; people's nostalgia rewrites their pasts.

————꙲⸲⸱꙳————

Everyone has had the experience of needing to recall something in a timely way. Often the answer is right there but other times it is just infuriatingly beyond our reach. We immediately look for clues to locate where the memory lies. If it is a name we seek, we strain to see the person's distinctive facial features, we search for an association with that person, as well as the context. The expression "so close that I can taste it" describes the search for sensory details in a memory retrieval.

As a concert violinist, I think about memory often. Conventional performance practice expects musicians to memorize our music if we play alone or as a soloist with an orchestra. Many schools and competitions require auditions to be presented completely from memory; anyone who has spent enough time with a piece of music to memorize it could be a serious and competitive candidate. With this expectation lying on the table for young musicians, even those who have been trained by ear—in the popular Suzuki method, students learn by ear before learning how to read music—memorization can be a stressful experience. We might spend months and years working on a piece, but when we get onstage we fear we will forget where we are, embarrassing ourselves in front of an audience.

PLAYER 1: How is your memory?

PLAYER 2: You know it's not good! It takes me forever to memorize, and I'm scarred by what happened at last year's recital.

PLAYER 1: You were fine—you stopped for a bit in the Bach, that's all.

PLAYER 2: It took me eight seconds to get back on. And eight seconds of silence and scrambling onstage feels like years. For the rest of the piece I was worried I would mess up again. I couldn't think about anything else.

PLAYER 1: That happened to me in a competition a couple of years ago. I got so confused that I had to ask the judges if I could see the music. They didn't advance me to the next round.

PLAYER 2: But you are so good at memory! You seem to have
a magic switch in your brain.

PLAYER 1: It's not like that. Memory is not as hard for me as
other things, like vibrato, but it is still a challenge.

Memorization comes naturally for some, which can give them
an edge in the early stages of studying an instrument. Others
have different gifts, like an innate sense of sound, or physical ease
when playing fast notes. Musical prodigies seem to arrive in life
with already-developed abilities, and memory can be one of those
notoriously mysterious traits. But as musicians continue in their
studies, those who persevere through their early struggles with
memory find themselves on equal footing with the people who
never questioned their abilities. And conversely, those who never
had to work at memorization have to spend more time on it as the
musical complexity increases. Using helpful memory techniques
(like inventing words, singing, constructing worlds of objects or
colors in one's mind) can turn anyone into a memory champion.
We search for resources to manage our challenges.

Students of the tabla, a drum from the Indian Classical tradition, learn the music without written scores, sometimes also without touching an instrument for years. A student initially speaks the
complex patterns and rhythms; once these become fully internal-
ized, the student is allowed to put their hands on an instrument.
This training seems to produce super-human performers, as the
musicians effectively harness their powers of concentration and
focus. A feat of the brain and the heart.

Memory recall in performance is linked to how those memories entered us. This associative memory is one of the strongest

sensory tools we have. It is what helps me to enter the scene of a dreamy first kiss, or to recall each second of a car accident years after it occurred. This kind of memory is often underrated by classical musicians. We are so obsessed with cataloging the tiny details of music on a ground level—notes, dynamics, markings, phrase shapes—that we forget we also have to build up a different level of meaning with it.

I have powerful memories of playing Franz Schubert's "Death and the Maiden" string quartet in formative years of my life: when I was age fifteen at the New York String Seminar, and again two years later, the summer that my former string quartet, the Chiara Quartet, met. The profound nature of my time as a teenager with the Schubert was key in helping me to commit the forty-five-minute-long piece easily and reliably to memory later in life when my quartet, now professional, started to memorize our music together. In the midst of playing the Schubert onstage in my 30s, I found myself in a wild space where the musical details were in the back of my awareness, and my sensory mind, influenced by all of the times I had played the piece, was front and center, leading the musical direction.

This kind of astonishing memory recall was hard to identify in all of its parts. My struggles with memory have been relatively few, but I figured the adroit Schubert memorization was due to years of growing up with the piece. All of the kinds of memory upon which musicians rely were there: kinesthetic (muscle memory), aural (hearing the music), visual (seeing the music on the page), structural (having a sense of the music's shape and order). But something else was a part as well, an indescribable emotional investment with the music made up of each performance I had ever given. Every note and phrase had meaning for me; it was a kind of complete bodily performative memory. I would venture to say this kind of memorization also harnesses the power of nostalgia.

———

There is a difference between nostalgia and memory. Nostalgia is emotionally driven, resulting in vague, sometimes inaccurate facts and details from the past. And since nostalgia involves longing, our dreams and wishes play a large role. I attended a James Taylor concert at Tanglewood in the 1990s at which the sky opened up dramatically halfway through the evening and all of the people outside, suddenly soaked, cheered and danced in the rain for hours. At least that is what I remember. But could my general nostalgia for the severe thunderstorms of those western Massachusetts evenings have affected my recall? Perhaps it was only for a brief moment that there was a storm. I can't imagine that I would have stayed outside in the rain for an hour or two. Memory, for me, suggests more faithfulness to reality. When constructing something from memory, the details matter—from an event's careful reconstruction in a legal argument, to the recitation of a dramatic monologue. The idea of memory suggests concreteness whereas nostalgia implies a hazier, more subjective recall.

Nostalgia's aforementioned crippling effects are found in musical performance experience. Many of us musicians, especially interpreters of older music, perform the same pieces many times throughout our careers, as I have with the Schubert. We often remember quite clearly the first or most meaningful time we played a significant piece of music (like that first kiss). A friend of mine decided to become a professional pianist after learning Brahms's monumental C Minor piano quartet at the Round Top Music Festival. Almost every time she hears or plays that piece she is transported momentarily to 2002 in the steamy Texas hill country. Trying to recreate that specific performance, however, can affect the tenor of her expectations in future outings.

If anyone holds on too much to the feeling of playing in a bygone heavenly environment, it can be almost impossible for that person to exist in the present. It is unfairly difficult for the other musicians who are trying to open their hearts to the music, right now. I have had many unpleasant rehearsal experiences from both sides of this problematic position: as the nostalgic one and at the receiving end. An example:

COLLABORATOR 1 (OUT OF 4): We all agree that this is the most incredible moment of the entire piece—we all love it. But it feels like we're not equally contributing to the intensity.

COLLABORATOR 2: We're trying. We've literally spent the last hour trying that "spinning thing" with the sound that you brought up . . .

COLLABORATOR 1: I know, but it's just not there yet. I don't want to be difficult, but we've all seen the video . . . and honestly that's exactly what I'm going for. I wish we could play it with real magic, like Sarah did in 2007.

This re-enactment may seem comical, but it's a more accurate rehearsal portrayal than one might think. Musicians feel things deeply, and it's quite challenging to bridge the time gap in any scenario in which another person is constantly lifting up the past.

So why would we imagine that this potentially destructive thought pattern could help at all with memory recall? Nostalgia seems like something to be avoided rather than valued. Why would I feel the need to revisit the past when I don't have to? Maybe I can learn something from a previous experience. Maybe I can locate when I had a meaningful encounter and how that shaped me as a person. Once I am reminded of the power of past times, I can make a commitment for the present moment to become life-changing as well.

Since music is a time-based performance medium, musicians often run into the issue of subjectivity. How we *feel* in any moment is of course wholly personal, and what we *remember* from a performance is based on many inner and outer factors. My string quartet competed in the Paolo Borciani International String Quartet Competition in 2004, playing Beethoven's quartet Op. 59, No. 3 in one of the final rounds. This piece was the most technically exposed work we were performing at the time, and we had been rehearsing with the goal of releasing the technique in the service of the music (i.e., not letting the hard stuff get in the way of playing freely).

Our performance in the competition round felt effortless— I recall lightness, like I was hardly working at all. All four of us agreed backstage afterwards that it was a special moment, and we were almost in tears. I was eager to listen to the performance of the Beethoven, since it had felt so otherworldly at the time. Did it sound the way it felt? Although we remembered a transcendent experience, upon listening to it we were surprised that nothing sounded particularly miraculous. It was a breakthrough moment for my awareness, and I like to reference that competition when people talk about how a performance *seemed* one way or another. As the great recording producer Judith Sherman reminded my quartet many times in the midst of recording, "it's not how it feels."

When I know a piece really well, I can distinguish between knowing it "by memory" and "by heart." For me, knowing a piece "by memory" means relying on the detail-oriented part of my brain to help me through a performance. I am actively thinking while I am playing, working hard to remember specific notes, phrases, and places in the music. Playing a piece "by heart," on the other hand, means that it is as integrated into my being as a childhood song; I have no fear of forgetting it or losing my place.

In "by heart" performances, an odd balance between what I am currently doing and what I already know settles in. My Schubert quartet experience is the perfect example of this present moment/ past reference awareness: I was simultaneously in both states of being while onstage. But we cannot grow up with every piece of music, so the goal of memorization for me is the nostalgia-making process of crafting meaning with a piece. This is about getting into the head of the composer so fully that I understand and love the music as if I had written it myself. I create moments through the learning process that make the piece stick, that make me a storyteller. Yet how do we make meaning in our memorization work without risking too much nostalgia?

———~୭

In the last few years of the Chiara Quartet's eighteen-year career, we worked tirelessly to learn many string quartets "by heart," and we developed elaborate ways to do so. We memorized and performed over twenty-five pieces, including the complete set of string quartets by Béla Bartók and Johannes Brahms, as well as newer works written for us. The initial memorization process was ideally a practical, unemotional one: we repeated short passages patiently as a group, mixed with analytical and structural work in order to know more deeply the composer's intentions.

We also sang and moved. I can recall exact days of the week, their weather trajectories, and rooms in which we rehearsed sections of Ludwig van Beethoven's Op. 132 quartet because of the way we sang it together. On one day of a memorization retreat we rehearsed in a university room with giant windows. As we intoned Beethoven's chorales together in the iconic slow movement, a storm started building outside, and violent gusts of wind lashed the tree branches against our windows in advance of the driving rain. The sky outside turned a dark gray at 3 p.m. as we sang on.

After years of performing long programs of quartet music "by heart," I became accustomed to playing without a score in front of me. I felt more comfortable onstage without the physical music. Something wondrous happened when the memory was solid: since I had already gone through the arduous process of deep learning, I felt free to be both expressive and more aware of my colleagues in performance. Music felt fully communicated, fully "by heart."

The act of creating memories beyond what is on the printed page—those emotional and meaningful details that stick—is about inventing context. This memory work is the most creative and personal. It's drawing pictures, making maps, singing and dancing, like reconstructing a piece from the upside down. For example, working on Missy Mazzoli's "Dissolve, O My Heart" for solo violin (a work that references an earlier piece, J. S. Bach's great D minor Partita for solo violin), I tried reorganizing the music, experimenting with what Mazzoli *could* have written. This wasn't intentional at first—after traditional memorization techniques didn't work, I decided to reshape the unique parts back together. The act of recomposition helped me to figure out what the composer chose to do, and I developed even more respect for Mazzoli's work.

Similarly, while memorizing Suzanne Farrin's "Time Is a Cage," also for solo violin, I rewrote the way the music looked on the page in order to memorize it effectively. I translated the musical rhythms into shapes—triangles, squares, circles, slashes—each representing unique material, so that when I tried to play sections of the piece I felt the music more spaciously, like a dancer might. The act of conversion into a different system opened up my imagination, like copying one's own notes again with a different colored pen, or singing a piece using a different language, like *sol fa* syllables. The learning process was playful and built memory quickly.

Memorization can resemble an odd step-by-step perceptual process in time. It requires us to move forward in order to better know a piece, then look backwards to check what we know. In memorization work I distinguish between learning, reviewing, and solidifying, all three necessary steps towards excellent and dependable recall. It is a kind of dance: two steps forward . . . many thoughts backwards . . . continual refreshing forward . . . then backwards again . . . only to head forward. Each performance is a daring flight with our memory work acting as the lift.

When discussing this conceptual process with a friend, she said memorization work for her does not connect at all to nostalgia. Her goal through memorization is to know the shape of a piece more and more each day. We develop fondness for what we love and with whom and what we have spent time, but building up memory for her is a way to recall the outline of a work of art and how it becomes more distinct with time and work. Knowing a work's shape feels similar to the act of any kind of creation or recreation, like putting together a daunting 1,000-piece puzzle or gradually adding to a painting. Each puzzle piece or stroke with a paintbrush contributes to refashioning the larger whole.

One of the reasons my quartet memorized the six quartets written by composer Béla Bartók was to relate to the ancient oral tradition of folk music that inspired Bartók's composition. We were strongly influenced by recordings that Bartók and his friend, composer Zoltán Kodály, made in the early 20th century of folk music from Hungary, Transylvania, and northern Africa. The performances on these recordings (captured on an Edison cylinder recording device) are notable for their lack of self-consciousness, something with which classically trained musicians struggle. Throughout the memorization process my quartet aimed to get closer to the world of these folk musicians who inspired Bartók's writing in the first place. In the oral traditions of earlier times, the collective, societal memorization of stories and music brought people together.

Longing, within reason, is a means to memory. I would like to think that the process of learning material "by heart" brings us closer to how we respond to art in the first place. Performing artists spend hours rehearsing moments of emotional virtuosity so that they can remind us of the extremes of our humanity. In this way, all art accesses the nostalgic impulse. It is up to us how we carry our longing into the future.

the beast of limitation

My left hand looked ghostly in the granular darkness. I could just barely see the miniature folds of skin cushioning each knuckle and joint. The thin tendons underneath the skin flexed and released in perfect conjunction with one another while I stretched my long and flexible fingers. Holding up my left and right hands, I saw that they were a marvelous pair. Even the crooked shapes of my thumbs bending and straightening in double-jointed postures were lovely in their own right. When was the last time I had looked at my hands in this way? Usually my gaze on these body parts tended towards judgment and disapproval.

I let my right hand fall down on the blanket, but kept up my left for closer inspection. The skin was draped across bones and muscles, appearing clearer and more active as the early morning light grew. I was well acquainted with this body part; as a singular physical entity, it bore outsized responsibility for my creative expression. My fingertips kept padded callouses after decades of pressing down my violin's metal strings. My vibrato colored the shading of a musical line, and where I placed my finger on the string achieved a specific density of sound. These intimate artistic choices all fell to the actions of my left hand.

———

The neurologist stood up from his desk and looked into my worried eyes with kindness. "This won't hurt," he said. "But I will need you to try to give over your control to me as we do these tests. It's much easier for us to tell what's going on inside your hand when you actively try to release any tension you have. A few deep breaths may also be helpful."

I nodded, and he stood up to prepare the machine. I sat on a table with my left hand spread out, the panic of the unknown rising high through my breathing. I was experienced at hiding fear. Nurses had always marveled at my low heart rate and blood pressure in routine checks. It was the opposite of white-coat syndrome—I went into a kind of catatonic state to combat my nerves, even though that calm was rarely present for me in performance onstage.

As the first jolt of electricity shot through my pointer finger, I jumped a little, almost recoiling, but remained still. Keep it inside, keep it inside. The sensation was like the charge felt from an accidental encounter with an electrical socket, but more directed: the machine knew exactly where and how far the electricity was headed. The doctor was right—those zingers didn't hurt. He picked up the clip and clamped it down on my middle finger, repeating the same process. On and on he went, until the clip was on the left side of my wrist. Right before the shock was delivered, I had a sudden image of my hand snapping off at the wrist like a plastic doll's, rolling underneath the table to accumulate dust with a used latex glove.

At first, I thought the mild, tremor-like motion would go away. Maybe I was just imagining it. It would disappear as other fantastical ailments had, like a tickle in the back of the throat whose concern falls away with soothing vitamin C drinks or is distracted by other more pressing needs. There was no pain in my left hand—it was just an inability to control certain fingers, especially when my hands weren't warmed up. A flutter or shake, imperceptible to others but noticeable to me. A finger sometimes couldn't stay fully down on the violin strings, and forcing it to do so created tension.

I was terrified by the idea that my physical technique on the instrument might be changing. I was only in my 30s. I knew that my precision would eventually fall away, but I was expecting this to happen after a long career, when I was much older. The unexplained erasure of physical, expressive abilities was like a specter of slow, early death. I knew people who had to leave their careers in their 30s and beyond due to focal dystonia, a neurological condition that muddled their control. Chaos and grief entered their professional lives.

The left hand of an older violinist I knew had curled inwards due to dystonia—the ring and pinky fingers were permanently folded into his palm from overuse and tension. His brain and hand could no longer coordinate with one another; at a certain point he stopped taking his violin out of its case.

———~♪

In my petite, low-ceilinged basement studio with a built-in bookshelf and red rug, I put together lists of specific left-hand violin studies that would build up my strength in a small-muscle-Olympian way. Single, slow trills, followed by sliding up and down the fingerboard one finger at a time—I gave these simple assignments to students to monitor their tension, and I knew they could help me too. After warming up, I moved on to an etude by Rodolphe Kreutzer and repeated passages five times slowly . . . then three times a little faster . . . three times again a little faster . . . three times slowly, again . . . two times faster, again.

But I kept getting distracted by stomach-clenching thoughts. What if I couldn't play dependably anymore, and what if my dignity as a musician was lost? The more I studied my hand the more frightened I became. Passages from a string quartet I had played since high school sounded awkward and irregular. My second and third fingers seemed to be losing their muscular clarity. It was all happening without reason—the degeneration of the violin technique I had built up over decades disintegrating within months.

———~ઝ

Back on the office couch, I scribbled down one of the doctor's phrases in my notebook. He continued, "But of course, there is nothing obvious. No visible dystonic posturing, as we discussed, and no nerve or muscular blockages, at least from what I can see right now."

I looked up, startled.

"You mean, you can tell me that with assurance?" I asked, incredulous.

"Yes," he said. "When I'm working with performers—musicians and dancers mostly—I often see some mark of their profession in their physical presentation. That comes with the trade. But these initial tests have turned up clear for the inner workings of your hand. We'll see more from the MRI soon. Perhaps there's something going on in your shoulder or neck that I can't test right now."

When I had read about the neurological issues I could be facing, my symptoms didn't entirely line up. Many who suffered from focal dystonia reported involuntary muscle spasms and erratic twitching. My symptoms involved an almost tremulous kind of energy, which sometimes worked to my benefit, helping to enervate my slow vibrato. It seemed to act up when I was feeling cold or emotionally vulnerable. Maybe I was dealing with something that couldn't be explained by a specific neurological diagnosis. I was still playing at a high level, but small and large psychological setbacks sent me into quick shaking.

———

While awake and asleep, I dreamt for days of being locked inside a cold, hard chamber surrounded by an unbearable clanging noise. I would escape the technician's grasp, run for the door, rip off my hospital gown. But my imagined claustrophobia turned out to be more invasive than the actual experience of lying in an air-conditioned, well-lit MRI white tube with headphones on. The space wasn't too enclosed, and the affable technician was a neighbor of mine. Thirty minutes passed by without panic.

———

A coach with whom I was working at the time asked me to imagine the energy of my left hand and what that part of my body needed to hear. I closed my eyes and dove into my hand, felt her timidity and isolation, her empathetic sensitivity to the energy of the room, her intuitive reactions to others. The years of nervousness, the physical expressions of anxiety—cold/hot/sweaty/dry/shaky/frozen—wondering if I was good enough to be on that stage; leading this or that group; playing with those super stars of the classical music world. All of this complexity was trapped in my quivering hand. The high energy inside ran fast and light. If harnessed, though, perhaps it could burst out, be transformed—creative, juicy, intrepid.

I still couldn't believe all of my test results had turned up normal, including second opinions I had sought. No signs of nerve damage or dystonic posturing in my body; no essential tremor; no muscular or nerve blockages in my shoulders, neck, or arm. But then what was happening? How was any of this "normal"? Because the stress and anxiety were very real.

Other players around me seemed to be thriving in the well-earned life of regular concertizing. They were known entities in the performance world who no longer had to prove their worth. Given my many years in the profession, I may have appeared to fall into that category too, but instead of building up comfort, I was growing more uneasy.

———

My hand was calm, my posture was strong and straight. I warmed up onstage with a violin I was borrowing from a prestigious instrument collection, and its sound resonated throughout the famed hall. I held the stunning, impeccably crafted violin from centuries earlier in my hands and felt its gift. The varnish was deep, burnished, and glossy. I hardly had to touch the strings with my bow for its glorious voice to radiate, reaching every corner of the room. The day before I had been concerned that this instrument of luminescent quality would lay bare my left-hand weaknesses. When I first tried the instrument, my nervousness presented as a tremor, obscuring cleanliness in Mozart string quartet passages. I hardly slept that night, worrying that the violin would be my unmasking. Yet the next day, I enjoyed the violin's warmth. Maybe I could smile a little as I played, releasing my anxiety into the gorgeous sound.

I lay in the darkness, up before the sun, practicing passage after passage on the bed sheets. All I wanted was for the concert that night to be over. Struggling mentally and physically during those days of rehearsal and preparation, I conceded that the best I could offer were just the notes. Trying to play beautifully had to be enough—I couldn't also promise to be emotionally open. I would go onstage and play the great violin, and I would monitor my left hand. It was about getting through.

———꘎꘎———

Heart quickening, stomach agitating, I skimmed the words again while chills of horror and shame cased through me, prickling on my skin like drops of cold water in hot oil. My sound was unappealing, my playing was inconsistent, my leadership was weak . . . Precise insecurities in print. The reviewer of the concert had not liked the conception of the program, including a world premiere, but I had seen plenty of those kinds of reviews. What was different was illuminated right in the center of the phone screen, enlarged by my panic: the reviewer had singled me out, multiple times.

So the magnificent violin had not in fact hidden my weaknesses. Showing up onstage and doing my job had not been enough. Everyone else had escaped ridicule, but I was marked as inferior. Other times I could have shrugged it off—maybe the reviewer simply had a bad night—but in this case I believed the reviewer was right on. Sitting in the running car, holding my cold phone, I was just a few steps across the dry, crackling snow to the warm lights of my home. My young children would want to see their mother, gone for a week. But what could I give them? I had failed. Also: I was done, I could no longer be trusted to go onstage and perform. My playing was proven to be subpar. I put my head down on the steering wheel and sobbed.

———ᵔ৶

It is hard to fairly describe the pressure involved in the classical music profession. Perfect intonation, flawlessness of tone production, excellent clarity of bow stroke and left-hand passagework are just a few expectations for any concert violinist playing at a high level. And it starts young—we learn through a system that rewards a right note over a wrong one, a beautiful tone over one that contains any scratch or whistle. Even given the supportive guidance of teachers, parents, and learning environments, studying an instrument celebrates perfection as a real, attainable standard.

In the midst of questioning my physical health and fearing I would have to stop concertizing, the strain of a lifetime of these expectations was almost too much for me to bear. In addition, I felt I had let down my group. I could not imagine how I would continue.

———ᵔ৶

It was like swimming, but through the air. Was this flying? All I had to do was bend a knee and I would lift up easily. Moving my arms pushed me forward a bit, but my legs did most of the motion. Sometimes I hovered in space, just above the ground.

This dream had first appeared a few days after I came home from my trip and read the bad review, and I couldn't bring myself to play the violin. Every time I went downstairs to practice I stopped right before sliding open the thin wooden door to my practice space. I felt too full of guilt and disgust to play. Since the doctors had no explanation for my condition, I blamed myself for not doing enough work, for not being able to isolate my physical problem. As snow and ice built up around our home, keeping us indoors, I fell deeper into a world of insecurity.

———⌐～ჳ

Tibetan Buddhist tradition portrays charnal ground as a place where nothing grows. An actual and representative place of absolute zero. Bones lie about and living things go to die and decompose on the desiccated earth. Charnal ground practice asks people to sit in this place of desolation, meditating on how they can piece their lives back together. It is considered a blessing to be able to start anew from such a low place.

My anger and impatience when practicing had gotten out of hand. It was next-level kind of inner talk, damaging and inappropriate towards anyone. When I entered a room to practice the air became tight, fatigued, and caustic. The spaces themselves seemed to call out for purification from my sighs and frowns, my eye rolls.

———⌐～ჳ

The sound echoed around my studio, but this wasn't the sound so familiar to me: this was the ring of a bell. I waited to feel a tinge of resolve and excitement as the resonance cleared. Apprehensive, I began playing a simple scale, one note slowly transitioning to the next. The violin felt light and warm in my hands, the bow connected deeply in the string. But after about a minute I started noticing the crescendo of voices. Why wasn't my left hand third finger shifting smoothly like my second finger (how annoying)?

And going down the fingerboard my shifts were still so wobbly (after all of these years).

I immediately stopped playing and rang the bell again. This was my first attempt, and as I sat down quietly, cross-legged, in the middle of my small red rug, I was stunned. It had been two minutes—I had lasted only two minutes after first ringing the bell. Like making a wish on an eyelash for show, my promises in a new kind of practicing were fervent but empty. Reactions to playing a simple scale were extreme and overdone. I held my left hand in front of my face as it shook wildly.

In *Living Your Yoga,* author Judith Lasater suggests marking the beginning and end of every yoga practice with the ringing of a bell, making a verbal commitment to practice ahimsa—a refrain from harming any living being—one of yoga's main tenets. I felt awkward appropriating the practice for my violin work, as someone who had only happened upon it in a book, but I was out of other options.

———∽

A cellist's extreme sensitivity to cold causes her fingertips to go numb unless she warms her hands with heating devices before wintertime playing. A singer's dry vocal cords create an uneven vibrato in her voice unless she lubricates her throat with an herbal mixture before vocalizing each day. Perhaps the emotional expression of my left hand, however shaky and tremulous at times, was just a part of who I was and would require special care for an amount of time. I started to look at my left-hand symptoms differently.

I might have been reduced to calisthenics with the combination of chiming and violin etudes, but my fingers were sharpening in strength and my tone on the violin was changing and developing. After many failed attempts at self-kindness in my practicing,

I had realized the only way forward was to start speaking to myself out loud with gentleness and compassion. I had done this with others—students, children, friends, lovers—who were in fragile and vulnerable states.

I ran down to my basement room many mornings to open up my violin case and practice for twenty minutes before I had to leave for the day. I worked on music that had felt heavy for so long, trying riskier fingerings and phrasings like it was a sport. Could my choices be bolder, more virtuosic? I winced as I revisited a few passages from the Mozart string quartet, now lighter and clearer, remembering how fiercely I had berated myself in my practicing only a few months beforehand.

But questioning whether or not I would be able to continue playing had shown me solutions, even as it had brought me down. The red rug became increasingly softer under my feet as I built up to thirty and forty-minute sessions with the bell. My tiny studio with books and paintings was a community.

———◦———

I hadn't taken the bell out for a few months, so I tested myself to see if the sound still summoned urgency and meaning for me. But after ringing, the instrument's resonance fell flat on my ears. I wrapped up the bell in its soft purple scarf and placed it in its embroidered black silk bag.

Sitting down on the bed next to my violin and stretching out my left-hand fingers, I watched the muscles and tendons flexing. My hand appeared the same as it had during my worst realizations, though now I felt more respect for the mysteries it performed, as well as affection for its needs. In three years of this work, I had moved towards self-forgiveness.

No longer entirely bound up in unrealistic expectations for myself, I found ways to operate like a trickster, playing with the stuff of music and pushing it around. This involved rewriting the music to be more challenging to play: working on pieces at twice their tempo; practicing passages using the edgy sound of *sul ponticello* (the bow played close to the violin's bridge); re-fingering entire sections to be played on alternate violin strings. New roads to bravery, risk, and subversion (the good kind) appeared.

———

I could see a storm was coming, but I was unafraid. My legs were like easy rockets, carrying me upwards and downwards in space. I had flown all the way up to the clouds this time . . .

A friend told me our subconscious works on our desires and struggles while we sleep. Our dreams show us the edges of what we can comprehend, just a miniscule picture. As I took musical risks during the day, my nighttime counterpart accessed effortlessness in shooting up to the sky. Dreams gave me permission to experiment with freedom.

———

The marks of my life experience appear on and through me. As I explore ways to reshape and adapt my artistic practice to my changing body, I see how vulnerability has brought in wider opportunities. My left hand may never function exactly the way that it used to, but then again, was anything lost? Now I play with fearlessness.

notes for themselves

INVENTION

(for my children: shapeshifters, creators, persons outside the binary)

Perhaps humans' obstinate natures dictate how we manifest our creativity. We are determined to make something out of nothing, to survive when the odds look most dire. Hikers who fall down mountain crevices invent contraptions in minutes to haul themselves out, or to keep themselves alive.

Artists harness this resourcefulness to stimulate their work. In pushing the boundaries of expression, they discover outlets for deep human striving.

In the late 1980s artist Matthew Barney produced "Drawing Restraints," a multi-year, multi-genre project exhibiting what is possible when basic physical restraints are placed on the artistic action of drawing. In a set of videos, Barney is seen bouncing up and down on a trampoline with his thighs contained in bungee cords. As he jumps, he directs himself from one wall side to another, making marks as he can. His work is both the frustrating process as well as the final wall drawing.

Composer Sofia Gubaidulina grew up in poor conditions in the former Soviet Union, playing in the back of her house, which was a rubbish heap instead of a grassy backyard. In studying and writing music she discovered the world of sound without margins. "I looked up at the sky, and I began to live up there . . . This all arose from poverty, but it was such richness." For Gubaidulina, the act of being emerged in the sound facilitates her clarity. She assigns herself tasks—like improvising with percussion instruments from East Asian musical traditions to find ideas for a piece written for Western string instruments: the violin, viola, and cello. She transfers delicately played sounds on a xylophone into an equally delicate series of plucked notes on the cello.

Gubaidulina admires an earlier composer, Johann Sebastian Bach, for his inventive tools. Bach's music sounds exploratory, but it is highly organized. Like Barney and Gubaidulina, he worked within strict confines to create vastly original music. I enjoy picturing him at work, writing his fifteen Inventions and fifteen Sinfonias for the piano (known as Two- and Three-Part Inventions, respectively), experimenting with the stuff of music: lines, phrases, energies. The sixth Invention is an exuberant back-and-forth sequence moving in contrary motion. Bach wrote these thirty succinct pieces as exercises, tiny investigations. They are restricted in length, ranging from a little less than a minute to almost three minutes.

Emily Dickinson wrote her "envelope poems," or collected poetic fragments, on the back of envelopes or on the corners of pages. These limitations seemed to only enhance the poet's opportunity for poignancy.

Invention is found in a liminal space between dreaming and execution. The steps: first, listening—knowing the voice, daily. Next, curiosity—because why else are we alive, but to learn and experiment? Many throughout history and right now cannot pursue creative work, so honor the privilege. Persistence—in making, in seeking, in justice, in all things. Another necessity: willingness to fail—an inventor cannot fear being wrong. How much more could be made without terror?

Invention, whether alone or in community, is also a call to action.

Katastakwók Karavan is an installation made by visual artist Kara Walker and composer/pianist Jason Moran, comprised of a unique thirty-two-note steam calliope (the kind of steam organ heard for centuries on riverboats) and housed in a wagon covered with Walker's searing etchings. The work's aims are representation, perhaps also transformation. It acts as a monument to Africans arriving to be sold into chattel slavery in New Orleans, specifically in the early 1700s at Algiers Point on the banks of the Mississippi River.

The wagon was stationed at Algiers for one day in 2018. As Moran played "old-timey" music on the whistling calliope throughout the day, the experience honored "millions of ancestors, in a way that we don't know what we're about to touch."

All humans know limitation. Our uniquely incomplete lives guide us to the tools we use to heal the world, to fill the cracks. We cannot know the full impact of what we make and release. Maybe transparency and light are brought forth, a new way through.

# of balance and purpose

The street cleaner has just gone up the street. His vehicle's skirt of bristles has brushed aside the road's detritus for now. Those of us double-parked for alternate side parking have to act hastily when we hear the automobile's strange roar from a few blocks away. I let my laptop, comfortably resting in a crevice of the steering wheel, fall into my lap. I put the car in drive and pull furiously forward to get a spot across the street. Other drivers have been waiting for this moment too. We all inch forward in our jerking and lurching ways, vying for the few spots available. I am second in line, so I land directly behind our older Ukranian neighbor's 2003 Honda Accord with a rusted bumper. The rest of the cars fall behind me, adjusting a few feet here or there. Within a brief two-minute segment the new arrangement of cars on our street has been settled for the week. My elevated heart rate slows down over the next few minutes.

Before I open up my computer again I notice how others are sitting in their vehicles after this flurry of activity. Some are on their phones, one man stares out of the window. A thin woman in a roomy dress and blue slippers gets out of the car and begins taking belongings of hers inside the building—a laundry basket, a bag. Soon her three children with bright orange hair accompany her to the car, to help their mother transport an entire carload to their apartment upstairs. They bring endless bags of clothing and beach things indoors. When the car is emptied, the woman returns to the car alone and looks with trepidation up and down the street, perhaps waiting for someone. I want to tell her that the police-woman will not come, now that we have acted responsibly as a street unit. She has no need to discipline us.

I force myself to get back to work. The clock reads 12:14 p.m. Forty-six more minutes to write as I sit and wait for the 1:00 p.m. hour when I can vacate my car. For now the interruption is over. I am virtually alone. My kids are at school, I have a sanctioned ninety minutes to think, maybe more after I go upstairs to make lunch. It doesn't matter that the most focused part of my day will be sitting in the car from 11:30–1:00 p.m., interrupted by a momentary transition of parked cars from one side of the street to the other. I will use it. And I must use it, otherwise it will not return. Any hint of procrastination will not abide.

I am reminded of writer Mary Oliver's essay "Of Power and Time" and how she separates time into parts and values. She distinguishes between three types of selves that define her life. There is a first, initial self who was a child and still makes her presence known in slight ways, as well as a second social self who manages and responds to the tasks of daily living, relationships, and time-keeping. The third self is what rules Oliver's days as a writer, one which is "out of love with the ordinary," "out of love with time," one with "a hunger for eternity." It is this third self that guides art-ists and mystics in all fields who strive for the extraordinary. Her essay invokes the awesome power of creativity.

Oliver was known to get up early and wander in the outdoors, taking note of the changing landscapes of her familiar haunts. She writes about how the seasons altered her perceptions of the pond she frequented, how she observed creatures and their evolution, even how she raided a turtle's nest for eggs, which she cooked and ate with delight. Despite an abusive father and a complex family dynamic, she recounts having free reign to wander in her childhood, to sometimes skip school, all in order that she could explore without worldly considerations. This upbringing, at least through her description, was a rarified one, in which she discovered and exulted artists with whom she identified—Ralph Waldo Emerson, Walt Whitman, William Wordsworth—other writers drawn to the mysteries of the natural world. In her distinguished life, Oliver was able to pursue a path subservient to the creative spirit she so artfully defines.

Oliver posits that if one answers the call to an artistic life, continually listening and giving this call a voice, the more it will appear and deliver. The creative call she depicts differs from the eagerness to get started on an already identified project, or to learn notes to be interpreted in a piece of music. What Oliver describes is the undeniable urge to create something new that is desperately needing to be released, to move the world forward.

As much as I agree wholeheartedly with these truths of following a creative spirit, I also pause. For how many of us are these truths daily realities? For those of us with families, relationships, and careers that are unpredictable, open space and time are not always possible, even if we set up our lives for that kind of room. The first few times I read Oliver's essay I was almost moved to tears by her words. I was inspired to change my life, to follow anew the third self, the creative call. I took down notes, copied favorite phrases. When I read Oliver's essay for a fourth, fifth, sixth time, these lines at the end of the essay stood out: "If I have a meeting with you at three o'clock, rejoice if I am late. Rejoice even more if I do not arrive at all." The gist is, from my reading, that if Oliver is serving the higher call to creativity, she cannot be disturbed by humans or descend into the world of the second self who attends to the mundane: other people, obligations, actual time. We should be grateful to be a small part of the genius she is channeling. These words hit me all the wrong way. The more I reread them the hotter my face became. I was indignant, defensive, and angry. In speaking her truth, Oliver had left me out.

Throughout the essay, Oliver implies that those who do "ordinary" jobs (she gives the example of an airline pilot) are not privy to the creative spirit. She makes a stark contrast between these kinds of people and their vocations, and those who live for ethereal mysteries. I don't disagree with her that there lies an inherent difference in purpose between flying a plane and writing poems or conceptualizing a landscape, and the personalities of people can be reflective of their career choices. But who is to say that pilots cannot also be artists? And what about those of us who exalt the extraordinary in the everyday, in the raising of children, those who have creative lives alongside the challenges of family life, including those struggles and joys? Are we not worthy of this third self that beckons from inside?

Creating an environment in which I am ready to answer a creative call at any moment, as well as being able to act on it, is a daily feat for me. But it is not one about which I am necessarily unhappy. I lead a life that includes other people, that is rich with back-and-forth, that is flexible in order that others can have fulfilling lives alongside mine. I am talking about balancing community and creative life.

———

I was told as a child that it was possible to have both a family and a vibrant career. My mother vigorously and repeatedly assured me that my children would grow up with the example of witnessing their mother pursuing what she loved—that this lesson was invaluable both to me and to my children. When I was on the road regularly for work—calling my family every day to check in, crying after saying goodnight, wondering if it was worth it—I needed to reaffirm my conviction to have a career that necessitated my being on the road. My children would grow up to know the importance of following their passions, I reminded myself. My mother, an accomplished pianist, was adamant that her own daughters pursue their multiple dreams, partially because she had experienced prejudice for being a parent. She collaborated frequently with a woman who made consistent, disparaging remarks about her life choices in an attempt to diminish my mother's skills as a serious musician. (This same woman, later in life, had a child.)

The truth for me is that the minute after my first child was born, I was aware of having a larger purpose. I had spent so many years faithfully studying to become a better violinist, but when I had a child, my life suddenly roared into perspective. Life was thankfully less about me. As a result, I became a much "better" violinist and musician almost overnight, even though it might not have felt that way. Eight weeks after my older child was born I played my first concert as a parent, and the entire event was altered. Backstage there was a tiny person waiting for me, and in front of me lay a string quartet by Ludwig van Beethoven. Beforehand, the Beethoven would have meant everything, a formidable task requiring my entire being. No less formidable, now the Beethoven no longer inspired anxiety; it existed as another wondrous activity in a world that had become clearer now that I was a mother. The sky had widened—the performance was less personal, less about my specific execution. I was still humbled by the musical demands, but after we walked offstage a member of my quartet remarked, "I'm not used to this level of confidence from you." Having children was a turning point, as when any person recognizes an essential aspect of their place in the universe. For me, embracing all complexity, it includes children.

I have spoken to other artistic parents who, like me and my partner, also underwent marked artistic growth as a result of (tempted to say: in spite of) having children. Perhaps having all of our comforts and personal needs obliterated in the service of small people required us to snap into action, clarifying exactly what was important to us. It also helped us to lose a certain preciousness surrounding our art. You can think loftily of your artistic practice until a child vomits multiple times all over your clothes right before a major concert or talk—then everything becomes relative, and there's no choice but to move on. My partner wrote a book of poems on his sleep-deprived subway rides to and from teaching engagements after our first child was born. We didn't have the funds to hire someone to help with childcare, so for the first year of life we tag-team-parented through adjunct teaching and rehearsal schedules. His only time to write was when he was out of the house or when our child was asleep. Likewise, I studied musical scores on my subway rides down to rehearsals, and I devised efficient ways to use my practice time at home while my child napped. I remember attempting to practice in our one-bedroom apartment when my infant could see me through the sliver of the door. Even as a small baby she locked her large, hazel eyes with mine, desperately trying to connect, as if to say, "What could possibly be more important than being with me? How could you betray me with that wooden toy?"

There were and continue to be ridiculous times—practicing late at night using a heavy metal mute on my violin to keep my children asleep in the next room; managing terrible sickness and other emergencies; traveling to cities with my children without having childcare yet in place; negotiating daily teenage crises. I was slated to perform at a music festival the two summers I was pregnant. The first time I almost fainted on stage during the performance and had to be taken backstage to meet a team of medics. The second time I wound up in the hospital the morning of the concert with pregnancy complications and had to stay on bed rest.

Sometimes I haven't been able to play my best, and sometimes when I am at my worst—under-slept, preoccupied, desperate—it is music and artistic practices in general that save me. I enter the world of expression with more of myself than I ever knew I could muster. I have learned to adapt and grow—become stronger, need less—and it has been worth the struggle, as finding equilibrium between multiple anythings one loves always is.

I desire and romanticize unrestricted time, and I admire someone like Oliver who organized her life in order to make her world view happen. There is no more profound place than the solitary hours in which to work and listen. However, in deciding to have a family with a partner who is also a creative artist, to raise children who are growing up to answer their own calls—this constitutes a valuable responsibility as well. I would argue that busy and often chaotic family activity does not have to deter one from the pursuit of a fulfilling, creative life. In answering the call of Oliver's second self I have not eliminated the call of the third self; it is still active and perhaps more vibrant inside of me because it fights to be heard.

None of this is to proclaim that all artists must have children or partners. Mary Oliver had a partner for forty years. One never knows another's situation. Some artists are not able to have children or have not met a partner with whom they want to share their lives and possible children. Others fill the role of chosen aunts and uncles, stepping in for friends and relatives when they cannot be present, physically or emotionally. Everyone has a part to play. Some artists who have resisted or not been interested in having a family life declare that their best energy will be pulled from their art to their family, and they are not wrong. They may be happier without the bedlam. A well-known pianist lives in a home with an adjoining house for her partner. The two see each other often but there is a clear boundary between the musician and her social world, a demarcation she has placed between herself and the person she loves the most. And she is an extraordinary artist. While the tension between my social world and my artistic world is strong, I have found that it is ultimately a meaningful one.

I hope to share a life that includes multiple expressions of creativity, an alternative to complete and total sublimation to one's artistic practice, as much as I admire that level of commitment. I also celebrate a life—in the midst of sick days, school assignments, and being inventive about mental and physical space for everyone in my household—in which child-rearing sparks newness and stimulates imagination, furthering our experience beyond the everyday.

As I double-park on a New York City street waiting for the street cleaner to come around the corner, I know the creative call can be answered many places where there is purpose and intention, where there is focus and ingenuity and the will to listen. For me this is in cherished moments of solitude: early mornings, late nights, library time, residencies, travel periods. It is also hunched over a journal on the subway, sitting in my living room in between bouts of music, yelling, and laughter.

notes for themselves

CONFLICT

(for my children: shapeshifters, creators, persons outside the binary)

Conflict in music mirrors life's rhythms and cycles. We celebrate an implied consonant harmony amidst angularity and dissonance. Foreboding peeks through a mass of benevolent chords. In order to interpret and express musical drama, musicians are used to engaging in healthy disagreement with one another.

But communication can easily grow dysfunctional in a full-time group, like a string quartet. During rehearsals we make mistakes and say and do things we regret, and sometimes this can go beyond: slammed doors, years of misunderstandings. The saying goes, after all: a string quartet relationship carries all of the drawbacks of marriage without any of the benefits.

My former group started playing together as teenagers. We were devoted friends who shared meals and sleepovers after long rehearsals. It was no boundaries at first; quartet was everything. But with closeness comes testing and discord, and our clashes could be upsetting. As someone who grew up without tools to handle conflict, who was taught to actively avoid it, I was often

silent or defensive in my responses. Realizing I had hurt someone, witnessing unfair exchanges between others, receiving uncar-
ing remarks—all of this sent me into paralysis. Heart and stomach
sick. Addressing the discomfort in my soul required courage,
which I thought I didn't have. For fear of confrontation, I often
hushed up and left my opinions by the door.

The acclaimed Guarneri String Quartet members were known
for their blunt communication with one another. String quartet playing for them was not roses and chocolates alongside the
magic of Franz Joseph Haydn's music. They gave us windows into
their interpersonal dynamics through books and interviews. First
violinist Arnold Steinhardt relays his experience of performing
Beethoven's Op. 74 quartet for the first time. "I remember coming
offstage . . . saying, 'That was terrific!' and the other three looked at
me in absolute horror, crying, 'You don't know what you're saying!
That was just awful!'" The group members reportedly never traveled together and stayed at different hotels or on different floors.
Establishing boundaries between their personal and work lives
enabled their particular musical communication to endure; they
played together for over forty years.

At Plum Village Monastery in France, a Buddhist community
founded by monk Thich Nhat Hanh and nun Chang Khong, the
residents use a Peace Treaty to resolve conflicts between partners
and colleagues. The two-page document carries two sections, the
first for "the one who is angry" and the second for "the one who
has made the other angry." In this simple and profound set of sug-
gestions for resolving conflict lie some assumptions: speaking and
acting calmly at the right time, with respect, empathy, and humility, will bring parties to a place of understanding. Also laid out is
the truth of symbiosis: "As long as the other person suffers, I cannot be truly happy."

The Plum Village Treaty prioritizes respect and time. It acknowledges that some conflicts will not be easily left or resolved, even if all of the proper steps are taken. It also suggests that by bringing our vulnerability into the light of day, admitting our faults and waiting for others to hear us, we come closer to peace. Once we deal with conflict our easily scarred systems start to repair themselves and make room for breath. Life begins to be shared again.

After many years of playing together my quartet decided we could do better in our communication. We cared too much about each other and the music—we had to find more productive ways to address our conflicts. In our second decade, we started each rehearsal with a stand-up meeting in a circle and answered three questions: 1. What have we done (for the quartet business) since we last saw each other? 2. What are we going to do today? 3. What prevented us from doing our work?

The third question at first felt like a trial. Some days I didn't have anything to bring up. Other days I summoned the bravery to talk about interactions that had caused me to lose sleep the night before. Maybe the hurt would be easier to discuss in a new day.

Soon I realized that expressing what was troubling me led to a release of tension. My opening up also allowed another person to clarify their point of view. I started looking forward to our stand-up meetings to see what would be uncovered; wrongs and misunderstandings meant opportunities for resolution and transparency.

In imagining others' perspectives, in wrestling with each other, we battle fictional narratives of ourselves and others as beyond comprehension. These are exercises with mirrors, gazing at what we wish to be. Empathy casts a wider net each time we risk it. Conflict provides its own light.

the Plains

I

Our first stop was always the bow maker's shop. The space was reminiscent of a compact hardware store, yet instead of tools on the walls, skeins of white horsehair and string instrument bows hung from long, nail-like hangers. Two men were hunched over a worktable and hardly looked up when we entered. One was in the final stages of replenishing the hair on a violin bow. Holding both ends of the bow, the frog and the tip, he gently ran the white horsehair through a two-inch oil flame to bind the strands together. The fire hardly wavered in its circular, iron lamp. The other man chipped away at a small wooden block with a knife.

"Hello there," the second man said in a measured, clear voice, his face turning in welcome for a moment. My father walked over and patted him on the back, but not too hard to disturb his fastidious work. "Good to see you. I've got three bows for you," my father said, placing a long wooden bow case on a bench. "How about three hours?" the man asked, without looking up. He added, "You heading to Jacques's? If you see René, tell him I need that Tourte bow back, pronto." My father confirmed the message, and we left the quiet, well-lit room, a secret haven in which I imagined the bow makers were magicians.

Our second stop was a few floors up, a sprawling space fitted with imposing-looking chairs draped in velvet wraps. Thick, purple curtains hung from the windows, giving the room a dark, luxurious tone, and the odor of stringed instrument varnish was ubiquitous. I could linger in the gasoline-like aroma of instrument varnish for a long time. If I encountered this kind of smell somewhere else I might wrinkle my nose at it, but in an instrument shop it soothed me. I noticed a similar, sensual rush when inhaling the turpentine and oil paint in a painter's studio. These smells comforted me; I knew creative acts happened when they were present.

We checked in with the receptionist before one or more men wearing suits with colored ties and scarves rushed out from behind the door and embraced my father, giving him multiple kisses. "Ah, look who came with you this time," they exclaimed with heavy French accents, "your little girl," leaning down to pinch my cheek a little too hard. Both men reeked of cologne.

In a back room my father played his cello—an old French instrument with a lion's head on the scroll—for the owners of the shop, Jacques Français and René Morel. Both men were luthiers, highly trained craftsmen who repaired, serviced, and restored fine instruments. Both Jacques and René originally came to New York from France in the 1950s to work for the Rembert Wurlitzer Company, known for bringing the rarest European instrument collections to the States. While this shop sold some of the most well-known and expensive antique stringed instruments—made by Italian makers like Antonio Stradivari, Giuseppe Guarneri, and Andrea Amati—they catered to every serious string player. Musicians flew in from all over the world to get their instruments adjusted and repaired by Jacques and René.

"How does this feel? Too tight? You need a little more depth on the C string?" The French men asked my father to play the cello again, spending what seemed like hours making tiny pushes and tugs to the delicate wooden sound post lying inside of the instrument. My father played, then handed the cello back to them for further adjustment. "Not quite enough on the A string now—we just lost the brilliance." The luthiers were like surgeons tinkering with a patient's health, although the patient was made of wood, and over 200 years old. I sat silently on a plush couch, drawing and smiling if the men swore at each other. When my father's cello started "breathing" again, and after enduring more kisses from the men, we paid the receptionist and took another elevator ride downstairs. The sickening smell of the men's cologne seemed like it would never wash off of my face, no matter how much I tried to scrub it later.

Heidi at the sheet music shop was my favorite. She spoke in a low voice with a droll cadence and strong New York accent, and she was consistently kind to me. Not pandering and exhibitionist like the men upstairs, just kind. My father said Frank's Music had everything. They carried the most obscure musical editions from all over the world, and Heidi, Frank's daughter, was aware of each item. She was the ideal librarian: she chose her words carefully, and a funny comment could swiftly become stern. As she wrote down our requests on a notepad she questioned us and our selections with wry laughter, then moved without urgency to the back of the store. When she reappeared with our music, I leaned over the reception table to catch a whiff of the mysterious back room full of shelves of paper music: dry, musty, and inviting. I wished I could hide in there for hours, reading and drawing.

At this point in the day I dragged on my father's hand and asked "Are we done yet?" a few times, even though I knew there was one final stop. My stomach was growling and my head felt light, but this wasn't just from hunger—I was also irritated at having to go to my father's quartet manager's office, which carried a constricted energy. I couldn't see out of the white-frosted windows in the cramped room where I waited, and the office coffee pot smelled old and sharp, making my stomach acid turn. It was always too cold to be comfortable, and the receptionist snuck accusatory looks at me while I tried to draw. Her forehead, nose, and eyes had a squeezed quality to them as if her face might suddenly retreat and suck itself into her skull. I was relieved when my father emerged.

Finally freed from the confines of the room, we walked through the streets of midtown Manhattan to the Carnegie Deli, which was filled with people demanding to be served and wait staff yelling orders to the kitchen. As we stood in the entryway I looked around at the photos of Broadway, TV, and film stars lining the walls, each famous person in their own carefully curated pose. Women like Bernadette Peters wore fancy hats and sequined dresses, or highlighted their generous breasts in tanks and leotards. Men like Al Pacino modeled sensitive smiles, dressed either in tuxedos or simple T-shirts. Eating at this New York City institution, complete with unlimited crunchy sour pickles at the table, was a tradition for us, but its gratuitously loud environment was far from pleasant. As I remember it now, I could not wait to get to our afternoon walk in Central Park.

The first time I was alone in New York City was as a fifteen-year-old, participating in the New York String Orchestra Seminar. We stayed in a hotel on West 57th Street, indistinguishable from an apartment façade except for the bright yellow awning displaying the hotel's name. My parents agreed to send me off to the ten-day program as long as college students of my father's also attending the program watched out for me. During the day I stayed in step with the group of 15-to-22-year-olds in the West Village, rehearsing all day except for brief breaks in which I left the building to grab a cheese-and-tomato sandwich and a Snapple. At night I escaped the hotel to walk through the still busy city streets with my seventeen-year-old friend, usually ending up at an all-night diner. We ate thick slices of cheesecake with processed strawberries, mushy from sitting all day in a glass case next to the cash register.

My neck was sore from constantly looking up. The age of the towering buildings in Manhattan captivated me, the discordant notion that so many stone structures in the city had been in existence for decades and centuries, yet people were still using them daily. Taking the elevator in a building devoted entirely to musical instrument sales and repairs as well as acting and dance studios, I often wondered what its past life contained. What kind of trade necessitated the building's construction in the first place, and did any remnants of inhabitants' activities remain in the stone? Like others before me, I vowed to do whatever it would take to embed myself into the materials of the city.

The orchestra was conducted by Alexander Schneider of the Budapest String Quartet, a man in his eighties whose glasses enhanced one of his eyes so that it was noticeably larger than the other. In our final performance at Carnegie Hall on New Years' Eve, a vigorous rendition of Franz Schubert's "Death and the Maiden" quartet for string orchestra, my entire body vibrated with excitement from the back of the second violin section. Schneider threw himself into the music with the ferocity of a wrestler. His aesthetic sensibility was directed by the obvious contours of the music— "When the music goes up, you go faster; when the music goes down, you go slower"—although the outcome was more balletic and nuanced than his directions prescribed. Schneider lifted the air in musical climaxes and plied it downwards as the excitement receded, his one enlarged eye miraculously trained on his score.

Before the ending of the Schubert I looked beyond him and the penetrating stage lights to the sold-out hall, smelling the heat of young bodies around me, baking in the triumph of our combined physicality onstage. We played the furious ending of the Schubert, raising our bows and releasing rosin into the air as a cloud of star dust. The crowd erupted into cheers and I felt the ten days of artistic growth like an infusion in my bloodstream. Gazing out at the alert and wide night, I also thought I could never leave.

2

This was our new reality: a flat, almost treeless landscape with nothing natural or human-made to obstruct our line of vision. It was day two of a twenty-three-hour drive, and I was starting to see how the living world thinned out as we moved north. The sky was widening, and the wind swept away anything unnecessary from view—weeds, dried grass, dirt. After years of living in New York City, a place that was designed to be vertically impressive, my body started to adjust horizontally to the Plains as if to a level.

We had stopped at an Auto Plaza off of I-94 in Fergus Falls, Minnesota. As my colleague removed the gas cap to pump gas into his green Subaru wagon, I also got out of the car to stretch my legs. The mid-August air was dry and fresh with a fall-like bite, even though I was wearing summer sunglasses as protection from the glaring sun. I could see farmhouses close to the gas station surrounded by a thin line of trees; these looked deliberately planted as a shield against the elements. Even standing in front of the car I could feel the persistent gusts that had threatened at times to move our car off of the road. The metal gas station signs rattled in the breeze.

I ran my hand over our instrument cases in the back seat and could tell that the violin and viola were staying cool. We covered the cases with our jackets to keep them out of direct sunlight, but there was still the possibility that the cases could soak up heat. In feverish nightmares I reached for my violin, only to have it melt slowly into a pile of soggy wood in my hands, my bow bending like a liquid object in a Salvador Dalí painting. Even though I knew this distortion was unlikely to occur in real life, my dreams reflected how easily our delicate instruments are affected by their environment. Obsessively monitoring my violin in the back of any car had become a habit, in case heat caused the varnish or glue to become unstable.

My entire string quartet was concerned about moving to a climate and location without luthiers nearby who dealt with fine instruments. In the dry winter months I would need to humidify my violin inside and outside of the case so that the wood wouldn't crack. What if something dramatic happened to our instruments, like our bows breaking or our fingerboards falling off? What would we do? We had already looked into driving the five hours or taking the nine-hour overnight train to Minneapolis should we need fine instrument experts.

Safe for now, and with a full tank of gas, we got back into the front seats and fiddled with the dial to find Minnesota Public Radio's talk station. We listened to Minnesotans discussing the upcoming 2000 presidential election as we continued on our way north.

During the great flood of 1997, which destroyed much of the community of Grand Forks, North Dakota, our destination, the land was completely covered in water, like the lakebed of ancient times that was the Plains' precursor. The Red River of the North—so named because it runs north—every so often gets backed up by the ice jams in Canada and causes extreme flooding. In 1997 the overflow from the swollen river decimated entire communities. Their roads were washed out, and the passage to any town in the area was blocked by muddy, icy waters. We reminded ourselves that the town was still rebuilding itself three years after this epic disaster that required national and international assistance and cooperation.

The sky was blue and cloudless as we left Minnesota and turned onto I-29 for the final hour drive up to Grand Forks. I tried to envision what the land on either of the road would be like as an actual body of water, glistening around us in the afternoon sun as we ambled north. Could the sugar beets become unmoored from their roots in the fields, the whitish vegetables free to bob on the water's surface? As I imagined us traveling through a wide lake, I realized that if the river flooded again on that scale we would not be driving. There would be no road anymore, and it would be impossible to leave the region by car or even by plane. I wondered with a pang in my gut if imprisonment by water in a northerly city could be in my future.

Early in January of 1999 at 8:40 a.m., three members of my string quartet huddled in the lobby of the Crown Plaza Hotel in New York City. We were practicing greetings and making sure all of us had enough business cards: "Hi____, I'm a member of the Chiara String Quartet. We're currently graduate students at The Juilliard School, and we're planning to become a full-time group after graduation . . ." We had planned a few meetings with managers and presenters between the three of us, but we were mostly interested in connecting with friends and mentors, letting them know that our quartet, together since high school, was preparing for a professional career.

I was wearing new high-heeled black boots and a lavender wrap sweater that made me look older and more authoritative than I felt, which was helpful for schmoozing with heads of arts organizations. We had planned to attend the first conference session of the day on community arts development, which included a panel of well-known urban arts leaders. Half-dozing through some of the session, I perked up when a representative from a New York-based organization made an off-hand, disparaging remark about the arts in rural America.

Suddenly I heard a pointed voice from the back of the room: "Excuse me!" I turned around to see a petite woman wearing a flowy blue and green tunic. As she began speaking with a clever and fiery delivery, she stood up so that more people could hear her. She said her community prioritized musical study. "I am the Executive Director of the Greater Grand Forks Symphony Orchestra, and in my city, more children play instruments than hockey, thanks in part to the Symphony's efforts." The director went on to counter with fierceness what the New York representative had said about rural communities, then she sat down. Captivated by her arguments and intensity, some of us clapped. The New York representative nodded and made a few muffled apologies, then the session continued. All three of us eagerly sought out the director afterwards.

We first heard of the Rural Residencies Program from the Ying String Quartet, who had lived and worked for a short time in an Iowan town of 600 people. This program was a unique (and now defunct) experience for a young chamber music ensemble to be in a rural community for two years. Initially championed in the 1980s by the National Endowment for the Arts, the Rural Residencies Program aimed to provide musical exposure and growth to rural communities that did not have much access to professional live performance. No longer able to pay for the program's expenses, the NEA passed it along to Chamber Music America, a national service organization devoted to supporting small musical ensembles. CMA pledged to keep the program alive with a stellar group of partnering organizations ranging from public school systems to colleges to community arts organizations in rural areas of states like Texas, Iowa, Oregon, Maine, and North Carolina.

When my string quartet applied to this program early the next year, we initially dreamt of being matched with a hamlet in Maine. We could live within driving distance of some friends and family and remain connected with our East Coast work relationships. But when we found out that we were paired with the Greater Grand Forks Symphony Orchestra, run by the woman who had so impressed us at the CMA conference the year before, we felt better about the match. Moving to the northern Plains to be a professional quartet was also the kind of challenge we desired at that point in our lives. Staying in or close to New York City would have scattered our ensemble's focus. We would have been pulled apart by the necessities of freelance life and making ends meet. And what could sustain our curiosity the way New York could, unless it was something diametrically opposite to the City: North Dakota? But as much as I felt ready to pursue creative life on the frontier, I also worried about how hospitable or livable the community would have to be in order for us to stay. Who would we become and what we would discover in the cold north?

3

After hiking up the massive earthen barriers on the western edge of the Red River, I stood for a few moments to admire the power of the river's flow. The brownish-gray water was full of danger in its northerly speed, although that may have been my projection; I knew its capacity for destruction. I was most acquainted with the calm waters of the broad Hudson River, which flows in both directions and flanks New York City's western side. From my view on the banks of upper Manhattan, the river's wide and peaceful motion rarely exhibited white caps, nor clearly detectable currents. The Red River's narrow width automatically gave the current a stronger and faster appearance. I compared these waters to flying in a small jet versus a 747 through the same weather.

Pictures from the Red River raging at its highest levels during the 1997 flood show muddy water so high that it covered homes and buildings and completely washed out streets. In a memorable photograph from the devastation, a dark green National Guard tank is submerged up to its middle with soldiers hanging out of the windows. They coast down Grand Forks's Main Street as orange fires blaze in surrounding buildings.

While locking the door to go out earlier, I could tell that this was a day when the town's two distinctive smells were on the air: one burnt, saccharine smell came from the American Crystal Sugar Company, which processed sugar beets south of Grand Forks (occasionally we would drive over a bulbous beet that rolled onto the road from the fields' tilling); the second vinegary, starchy smell wafted in from the Simplot factory in the north end of town. Simplot was a large provider of potatoes for fast food restaurant chains. I preferred the sugar beets to the potatoes—both odors were far from the oil-laden wafts of the luthiers' shop.

I had checked the wind direction and temperature on the Weather Channel before gearing up for my walk, but I was starting to learn that in early October the northerly wind rushed through the streets with force in many directions. A walk would either feel like a breeze or entail a fight to get home, depending on my relationship to the wind. Without much help from the weather experts, I brought a hat and gloves just in case, and headed down the residential street towards the river.

I saw no one as I passed older homes built in the 1920s and 30s, still standing strong despite the horrors the weather has visited upon them throughout the years. Even though the temperature was above freezing, balmy weather for early fall in North Dakota, it was not quite nice enough for people to be out and about. But maybe people didn't go "out and about" in Grand Forks. I was still figuring out the ways of the town. I had heard that once the snow started, everyone stayed indoors and baked pies and cookies for seven months of the year, rarely venturing outside. But surely it couldn't be time for that yet, and the baking stereotype seemed unlikely to me. Little did I know how extravagant the "bars" loaded with all kinds of sweet treat items—chocolate, butterscotch, cherries, marshmallows, nuts—would appear at every event between October and May.

A university professor had already chastised me for buying a new purple bike at Walmart. He shook his head as he saw me ride up to the school with my violin and bag slung across my back. "That was a waste of money. You'll only be able to use it for two months, if you're lucky." I pushed off my annoyance and laughed as I walked my bike indoors. But he turned out to be right: the first blizzard hit in mid-October, and the bike sat in my garage until the following May.

As I stood atop the river barrier, in a sudden moment of fear I imagined the river rising, expanding, engulfing my body and snatching me away. There would be no way to resist. The elements, unleashed, would have decided to claim me. I turned my face to the wind from the south and caught the acrid scent—sugar beets. My way back home through the barren streets would be accompanied by loose, dry leaves, a biting chill on my cheeks and hands, and a burning sensation in my throat.

———

In our yellow-walled, windowless studio at the University of North Dakota, my quartet unpacked our instruments, discussed a few business items, and opened our light blue books to chorales by J. S. Bach. Each of us took a different "voice"—bass (cello), tenor (viola), alto (second violin), and soprano (first violin). We played the solemn hymns slowly and beautifully, noticing intonation and sound blend, taking turns following each other: the viola led the first two phrases, the second violin led the third and fourth phrases, and so on. Often we decided not to designate a clear leader, encouraging responsiveness to the slightest of gestures.

Could we become one organism, one voice? We changed our sounds in miniscule ways while adjusting to each other—one morning I focused on the cello, another on the viola. We matched and differentiated until we were warmed up enough to tackle music by Claude Debussy or Gabriela Lena Frank. Could we listen with the same level of care and detail while playing these more complex works, full of devilish challenges, both individual and collective?

Our rehearsal process felt like it was happening in a vacuum unless we went into the community to perform. In a town two hours west of Grand Forks, we played at a school assembly full of students who had not heard much live music of any kind. We faced 200 people seated on a bright yellow gym floor with their backs to huge windows facing the prairie. A young boy stood behind the rest of the students, dancing throughout each piece, his feet moving noiselessly but continuously along the spongy floor. In between the music he raised his hand several times to answer questions we asked. At other times we saw him in conversation with his teacher. The teacher told us afterwards that this boy had never been so absorbed. He had begged his teacher, "Please, please call my mother and tell her to come over here, now!"

Later that night we peered out from behind the stiff, green velvet curtains before our concert at the local college, looking out for the boy and his mother. Had he convinced her to come? We tried to scan each person's face in the darkened auditorium, but with many people standing, we never saw if the boy and his mother made it to the show.

———

When I searched for the ingredients of a fulfilling life, I found them in my current situation: work right out of school, pursuing my high school dream of playing in a string quartet, living in a welcoming community, being housed and paid a living stipend. Every day I was aware of the fortune of my arrangement. Despite this objective goodness, however, I was constantly anxious and unable to sleep. A loneliness haunted me at every moment. I had trouble acknowledging this, given how often I interacted with people. Even indoors I felt naked, like the barrenness of the landscape was trying to get at me, to rip holes in what I had managed to keep intact. I wrapped myself in blankets in my cold bed, reading until the early hours of the morning. As the snow piled up and the blizzards descended without warning, I found little joy even in the routines that involved colleagues or new friends. I wished for warmth and home.

In *Dakota: A Spiritual Geography,* writer Kathleen Norris likens her experience of moving from New York City to rural South Dakota to that of the ascetic monastics and desert fathers who occupied remote and stark locations. So much of her perception and understanding had to change in order for her to fully embrace her chosen environment: "The western Plains now seem bountiful in their emptiness, offering solitude and room to grow." I read Norris's book while living in North Dakota and was inspired by her transformation, guided by the possibility of access to the prairie mysticism she found. Maybe I too could claim a poetic space and make art in an isolated location. What would I need for true happiness? If I could be fully present to my environment, perhaps companionship and peace were right in front of me.

In a particularly trying moment of the forbidding March winter, I made a visit to a counselor who seemed like a compassionate figure. She listened to me in earnest, and she sympathized with my feelings of loneliness, so far away from what I knew. But she had to admit that the space of the northern Plains gave her nourishment. The wide-open skies filled her, as they did for Norris. I marveled at her condition, still thinking: how could one be nourished in a place so punishing, so colorless?

For a while, I found solace in an obsession with extremity in general. I watched films about people barely surviving their Mount Everest climbs, read *Into the Wild* about the fatal Alaskan adventure of young Christopher McCandless who lived in an old, rickety bus for months and ate animals and vegetables off of the land. I cultivated an unhealthy nostalgia for the novelty of the landscape, the unforgiving quality of the prairie. The wind blew with no check. Daily battles with the weather blended together into a practice of existing in awe of the elements, and there was a part of me that feared, like McCandless, I would succumb to the land entirely. In having great respect for the animal that was unpredictable climate, I both worried and wondered if I would just vanish at some point.

My sister visited me during a warm spell in April, and we spent an afternoon watching films in the living room with the blinds drawn. Anything could have been happening outdoors. Close to dinnertime we opened the windows and saw that trees, cars, and homes were covered in dirt. The smell of dark and vibrant earth was ripe across the air. Cars in their driveways were completely brown on one side, as were the eastern facades of homes and retail buildings. In that short hour or two, a 100-mph windstorm had barreled through the area, marking anything standing with its unrestricted rage.

In this moment of being outdoors, the newly thawed earth woke and revived my senses. If pride is associated with a sense of home, I was surprised to find that as I introduced my sister to my current surroundings, I spoke proudly of the wind's force. For a few short hours I was in love with the materials of the northern Plains, even as they were serving me with fear and loneliness. Can one yearn for a situation while living inside of it?

4

The large and clearly distinct squares of farmland looked gentler and more verdant than what I had expected. From the plane window high above, I noticed slight hills, corn fields, and haystacks that reminded me of a Sicilian countryside, baked and dry in August from the heat of the summer, but still green. I was also grateful to see that trees in eastern Nebraska were taller and more plentiful than trees in the Dakotas. Later I read that the first American Arbor Day occurred in Nebraska City, less than an hour south of Omaha. On that inaugural day in 1872, residents planted an estimated one million trees.

As the plane descended, I looked at pictures I had printed out of our roomy two-bedroom loft. We rented it after seeing the space online and talking to the landlord over the phone, a far cry from the New York City broker hustle. The airy apartment with high ceilings would cost sixty percent of our one-bedroom rent in Manhattan, and our ten-month-old baby would have her own room. The top of our piano would no longer need to be used for diaper and clothing storage. I looked forward to walking out of our front door to a weekend farmers' market and enjoying the sun and more sun towards summers-end. Would our family spend nights gazing at broad sunsets punctuated by distant calls of Amtrak trains making infrequent stops? Perhaps in this more genteel Plains location I might find the opportunity for contemplation promised by Kathleen Norris, which eluded me in North Dakota.

I had visited Nebraska the previous summer, but my memories of that time were blurred by crippling, pregnancy-induced insomnia. I also thought I might die from heat suffocation. Being pregnant anywhere in weather that is consistently in the mid-90s with above-80-percent humidity is a challenge, but spending seven days in that weather in Lincoln, Nebraska, was excruciating. I crawled from one air-conditioned space to the next.

I lived for that week at The Cornhusker, a quaint hotel in downtown Lincoln with an unremarkable bar that served me milk and a banana for a night-time snack. Before my teaching and performing started for the day, I wrote letters to my partner with the blue ballpoint pen and old-fashioned font stationary provided by the hotel. I expressed my longing to see him and to meet our baby. I also described the differences that I saw immediately between Grand Forks, the Plains town that I knew, and Lincoln. The former (especially before its oil boom) was a remote outpost, one hour north of Fargo and two hours south of the Canadian border. The latter was a relaxed midwestern college town of over 250,000 people that touted a college football team of past glory. While the state of Nebraska seemed remote from a coastal perspective, the city of Lincoln was a healthy size. Life in Lincoln, even considering the destructive summer thunderstorms and tornadoes, was fair, not extreme.

One day that week my quartet drove out of town at 9 a.m., leaving behind bland housing developments and sidewalks for swaying prairie grasses. The tree leaves moved in accord with the grass, a relationship well-tested by the abundant (and steamy in the summer) breeze. In North Dakota the austere, flat landscape had conjured impressions of a wide, still lake. The Nebraska prairie, on the other hand, was about flow, a spacious land of growing things in constant motion.

We pulled up to a white church in the middle of the prairie with ornate stained-glass windows and a bright red door. I rolled out of our Jeep wearing the summery black dress originally bought for our baby shower, with a satin pink bow spread across my full belly. As I took my violin case out of the car I heard the sound of voices and laughter coming from the lawn in front of the church. A considerable number of people—families with children, adult couples and single adults all wearing helmets, exercise shirts, and shorts—were waiting for us with their bikes. A crowd had ridden out, an hour early, to hear a mid-morning string quartet concert. I knew the effort required to build audiences in North Dakota, New York, and elsewhere, and this group of bikers' dedication impressed me.

———

"It's the director of the UNL music school," our violist said, "hold on." He grabbed his phone and ran out of rehearsal to take the call. I laid back in the chair, closing my eyes and trying to rest in place. This conversation with the effusive administrator might take a while. But our violist was back in ten minutes. "Hey, guys," he said, "we need to talk." It had been a few weeks since our July visit to Lincoln, and the director was calling to gauge how seriously we would take an offer to move to Nebraska for a three-year residency at the university. The director was fairly confident he could raise the funding over the next six months, but he didn't want to try if we weren't interested.

A silence fell in our group after our violist delivered the news. We looked around at each other with wide eyes, mine carrying a trace of fear. My stomach, even compressed as it was by the baby in close quarters, flipped nervously. Could I bear more years on the prairie?

In theory, I wanted to be an artist who could exist anywhere, who could do my best work in any location. In reality, though, I was reluctant to leave, yet again, the place I had chosen as a young person. Living in North Dakota felt lifetimes away, only two years after returning to New York. I was in denial about who I had become while in Grand Forks, and I had no intention of going back to the person who had developed a fascination with, even a craving for, severity. The infrequent urge I had to recall my shadowy self was less wistful and more perilous, like an alien creature resting inside, better left dormant. I had also made a pact to reenter New York City's mysteries, to live with its dysfunctions, even as I questioned and pushed against them.

During two years on the prairie, I longed for the lush East Coast vegetation, the way the wind blows slower through forests. The materials of the land of the plains—wind, sky, space, corn, dirt—however marvelous in their own contexts, had stayed foreign to me in that particular landscape, even fearsome.

And back in New York City where I shared an apartment with my partner, I felt at home again. Our mornings began with a soprano's vocal warmups from the north side of the building; the clarinetist below us practiced a concerto by Wolfgang Amadeus Mozart that turned later into a Klezmer improvisation; on warm days the guitarist across the fire escape sat in front of his window and wrote songs. With my classical violin playing added to the mix, the musicians in my building created a Charles Ivesian soundscape, a quintessential New York City collage. As a young person I had dreamt about being part of this kind of vibrant, almost accidental artistic community.

My partner and I were committed to sustaining our social life, even though we didn't have much money. After writing friends in the morning about an evening dinner party—"We'll provide pasta, you bring everything else"—at 8 p.m. our apartment was full of yelling about news and art while drinking beer and eating an occasional cake someone had managed to make that afternoon. The festivities migrated from our main room to the fire escape, with a few friends leaning against the railings. My partner and I washed and dried dishes side-by-side in the kitchen, the warm light of lamps keeping us awake at 2 a.m.

My quartet was working so hard that I often forgot we still lived in a vast city. On days that we met for five-hour rehearsals, I walked through Fort Tryon Park between our apartments in upper Manhattan, returning home to write business emails and cards, and practice until late at night. These few blocks constituted my entire world for weeks at a time. But I was infinitely grateful to be able to play string quartets all day, to analyze music by Henri Dutilleux and Jefferson Friedman and emerge with wonder that the rest of life still functioned.

I thought about all of this as I sat facing my quartet colleagues, my pregnant belly rising and falling with quick breaths. To dampen my shock at the University of Nebraska invitation, I tried envisioning benefits of returning to the Plains: we would have more physical and psychic space, as well as health insurance; we could raise our child in a place with open fields and calm streets. But what would this mean for our quartet's rising career, for my partner's artistic life, for our unborn child's sense of home?

"Today a pea-chick died," my three-year-old said one day on the ride home from school. We were driving on dusty prairie roads behind a horse trailer. "We put the pea-chick back in the earth." She was sitting in her car seat, looking out of the window and speaking slowly. Then she began to sing in her high, clear voice. "Everything goes back to the Earth." I smiled at her in my rear-view mirror. Her days at a solar and wind-powered Montessori school on a farm twenty-five minutes outside of town seemed marvelous to me. "Everything goes back to the Earth." Even in blizzards and torrential rain she and her friends dressed themselves methodically in down layers, mittens, and sturdy boots, poured water for the ducks, collected eggs, and fed hay to the ponies. "The sun shines down." She tended the gardens with three composting stations, as well as planted and harvested vegetables, fruits, and herbs. "The rain falls down." She saw death from an early age as a part of life, as a routine. She was experiencing the wonder of the earth and developing her own mysticism in the ways I had as a young person, albeit in a different location. "Everything goes back to the Earth."

In Lincoln our quartet studio was a basement room with white brick walls, previously used as a tornado shelter. Sitting in the middle of the room in a circle with our musical scores and stands placed to the side, we played and sang; we listened to phrases of music together. In between playing I looked around at all of the stuff of our work life: recordings and concert programs piled high in a wooden cabinet; a library of music carefully categorized in flat files; personal teaching books next to an out-of-tune grand piano. As we repeated the opening phrases of Ludwig van Beethoven's Op. 133 *Grosse Fuga* for the seventh time, I felt the components of the music—dynamics, harmonies, phrase shapes—affixing themselves to me. There was nothing as challenging as this quartet memorization work. It required every inch of me, both mentally and physically. Part of the thrill was that in any piece of music the unknown would make itself more distinct the more we scrutinized it.

I was determined for every part of my life in Nebraska to prevail over my stay in North Dakota. In hindsight, much of my despair in Grand Forks could have been caused by a youthful lack of coping mechanisms to deal with loneliness and cold. Now that I was in a more southern, less extreme version of that part of the country with my family, I assured myself that life could blossom.

Sometimes my palpable memories of New York City felt like a noose, thwarting my attempt to create a gratifying life elsewhere; other times they felt like a welcome distraction to this fair existence. I struggled because New York was in my origin story, but I couldn't keep it too much in my present tale. I tried to convince myself that I was over the city, that I wouldn't be drawn back in again. Each time I left the Omaha airport at 6 a.m. and arrived at LaGuardia airport at 9:30 a.m. it was for quick business trips and performances. I stayed on friends' couches and went out for drinks after concerts. I tried to ignore New York's attraction, but when I had an afternoon off, I walked through the streets and parks, listening to the sounds of the city and enjoying the stream of people around me, pining to be there.

But mostly I noticed the city's myriad faults and challenges—the slog of public transportation, the expensive food, the airport stress. How lucky was I to live in a quieter part of the country where my work was a seven-minute drive from my house? Seeing New York City from the outside was like being in the arms' length phase of a failed romantic relationship with a co-worker. I had to keep the former object of my affection at a distance, even though we still worked together. Should I try to release my attachment to New York City for good?

5

A rush of birds flew in front of my windshield view. The group was fifty feet above me but seemed close. I could see each bird beating its wings laboriously, then flying low to the ground to alight nearby. I followed the birds' descent out of the window and almost drove off the road from surprise. The fields, normally greenish-brown or golden as the dried grasses and husks of last year's corn mixed with new growth, now appeared gray, almost white. Thousands of magnificent grayish-colored birds populated every available space, some rising briefly off of the ground to flap their wings or to leave the fields in groups.

I pulled off the highway and stopped the car. When I opened the door, the sound was tremendous: a chorus of cornet-like singing came from the birds on both sides of the highway, turning louder and more jubilant each time a small number lifted off, rising into the open sky. I had never seen the extraordinary sandhill crane migration before, but I had read that an estimated 600,000 cranes land in Nebraska each year. While the Platte River Valley has provided a space for them to roost for the past 10,000 years, several species of the cranes have been alive for more than nine million years. They are one of the oldest birds on the planet.

That morning I had left the crisp mountain town of Boulder, Colorado, to drive home to Lincoln, hoping to pick up my children from school in the afternoon. My partner and I spent our first wedding anniversary driving this same distance on I-80 across the state of Nebraska. We stayed with friends who own farm property on the border of Colorado and Wyoming and woke up early to the sun. A wilderness of rocks, wildflowers, and the smell of silver sage greeted us. After a morning hike along the arid landscape, we spent eight hours driving east, crossing the Cornhusker State and stopping at a diner just over the Iowa border for some celebratory cherry pie.

At that time in my life as a New York resident, driving for eight hours through only one state was extremely unusual—that kind of distance hardly exists on the East Coast. Eight hours north to south will bring you from Maine to Maryland, spanning entirely different climates. But now that I was a resident of the Plains, driving long distances was commonplace.

Seeing the cranes feeding and flying together on every available area of the fields stirred up a deep humility in me. In these creatures I saw two things that I was missing: a following of the earth's homeward pull, and the togetherness of a species. After living in Nebraska for eleven years, I still felt adrift and comparatively out of touch with my own inner wisdom. I thought of writer Joseph Campbell's observation that in our increasingly competitive society, the relationship between humans' collective conscious and unconscious zones have been severed; society has lost its fundamental value as the individual is prioritized over the group. Standing alone in the fields, viewing the rare occurrence of the crane migration, I wanted to be a part of something, to identify with my own group.

How could I learn to listen to forces stronger than my own temporary, economic, and vocational needs, perhaps hearing voices from generations or centuries earlier? I knew from studying religious traditions that communities in other parts of the world like

South Asia recognize soil to have characteristics that affect individual and family pasts. A physical location dictates much about a person or group's place attachments for the future. What soil was calling to me? When would I listen to this level of resonance and be "called home"?

6

As our enormous commercial moving van pulled close to the curb, we were anxious for a much smaller moving truck to finish loading. Both trucks together couldn't fit in the no parking zone on our block without backing up traffic for hours, so our large truck sat idling off to the side. Seven people ran quickly in and out of an apartment in our new building. They emptied the apartment's contents into the little truck and tied down furniture to stay secure for a long drive.

For a while I waited, leaning against the building and soaking up the mid-morning June sun. I smelled the strange combination of warm trash and sweet pastries from down the street. Then in an effort to speed up the loading, I decided to say hello to the group of self-movers. Perhaps not surprisingly, we realized we were all musicians and had probably crossed paths in graduate school. One of the drivers mentioned that he was moving to Lincoln, Nebraska. "We're ready for a big change. After twelve years in the city it is time to get out." Smiling, I told him we had just left Nebraska after thirteen years, and I hoped he would find the change he sought on the prairie. Physically and energetically my family was trading places with this man.

When my string quartet had finally run its course after eighteen meaningful years together, my family realized we had the world in front of us. We thought about living overseas, in Berlin, or moving to Los Angeles for the thriving visual art scene, a little wilder than New York's. We also looked into starting an interdisciplinary art school in Cambridge, Massachusetts. All of these options would require significant learning curves; we had never lived in any of those places, and it was time for a new adventure. For the first time, we weren't moving with my quartet's employment in mind.

As we researched work and flew to different cities, had job interviews and talked to other arts professionals, New York City kept coming up in conversation. A sixty-year-old friend and long-time New Yorker mused, "You can reinvent yourself at any age here." With hesitation, we started to reconsider New York, reaching out to connections and imagining what life would look like for a family of four with two arts professionals in our 40s. As every other option fell away and the city where we met and wrestled with our vocations for the first time reemerged as our primary choice, we asked what New York might have to offer us this time around.

I hadn't planned on loving the city again the way I had as a young person. I assumed that with no full-time employment I would collapse under the high-priced living. Coming from a suburban midwestern world of home ownership and afternoons spent driving my children to activities, I figured that the hassles of public transportation and apartment rental would weigh me down. Moving back to New York City felt like a dangerous, risky move to make. To reference writer Joan Didion, we were neither very rich nor very poor, and we also weren't young.

My family did our laundry every week a block away from our apartment; we drove around for hours trying to find street parking; we sat on trains stopped for delays in between stations; we waited, to no avail, for our building superintendent to fix ceiling leaks. All of these were daily challenges inherent to New York City survival. But I found I could navigate these. I was relieved to be rid of the neighborhood pressure to keep our lawn nice—I could spend that time walking in a park instead.

In reestablishing relationships with instrument and bow shops, I figured out who could help me in an instant with both regular and emergency repairs. While many businesses had changed ownership—the cult-of-personality dealers who kept a tight hold on New York stringed instrument life for decades had passed away or retired—some, especially bow shops, were entirely unchanged. Even if a physical place had moved, the energy and wonder inherent in the micro-work of rehairing and crafting bows remained the same. The smells of varnish, wood, glue, and rosin—relegated to my sensory nostalgia for so long—were once again part of my everyday existence.

Life in the Plains states ran in subservience to nature and her elements. But strangely it was in New York City that I noticed the abundance of vegetation unapologetically covering every available surface, erupting through concrete streets and challenging the human-made. The natural world's persistence in the city reminded me of the fight I felt as an artist in my communities on the prairie, frustrated at times by the responsibility to provide artistic stimulation—something I craved for myself—for students and audiences. But I had also learned how to make art without rules or boundaries. Artistic friends of mine in New York City had built successful lives all of the time I was gone, but these friends had not been forced to question their New York-centric view of the world and legitimize a life elsewhere. By myself and with my string quartet, I had created and weathered a rapid pace of rehearsal, performance, community engagement, teaching, and travel from my home base in Nebraska. As my sister-in-law noted on a visit to Lincoln, her first time out West, "Out here there are no rules—you make the rules."

———✿———

On a mid-June afternoon I entered Fort Tryon Park in upper Manhattan with my children. We walked slowly through the heather gardens, taking note of plants bursting in seasonal glory: three kinds of lavender—French, English, and Sea—all proudly exhibited their flowers and resultant aromas; the lamb's ear, big-hearted and soft, lay close to the soil; the basins of a few pink roses were still full with rain from an early afternoon shower.

We took turns sniffing the indulgent sweetness emanating from these flowers, reminded of a lone rose bush that persisted each year on the south side of our Nebraska house. In any given year the prickly bush yielded few flowers, but each appeared like a shock of pink lipstick against the house's pale, tan siding. Maybe at this moment the bush was already producing more flowers for the house's new owners; or perhaps it stayed resistant to all human efforts, not just ours.

We wandered out of the gardens, following concrete paths that twisted slowly upwards to the highest point of the park—a stone wall circling the river view. The grayish-blue Hudson River appeared calm and mighty between us and the bluffs of New Jersey. Its girth had to be at least a mile wide. In the distance, north of the city, the river gathered mist as the warmer air met the colder water temperatures.

I raised my face to the generous wind, closing my eyes and becoming aware of the fragrant earth pulsating around me. I thought of the gifts of the prairie—the space that is all-encompassing, the tempo that does not interrupt or rush. I might not yet be capable of relishing in the unrestricted view of the prairie sky for what it is, simply, without emotional attachment to my fifteen years of feeling like I didn't belong. But now that I was back in the city, perhaps accepting the Plains as a part of my personal lodging, my heuristic literature of place, did not have to be so arduous. Like the sandhill cranes, I had trusted my own pull.

My younger child looked up at my contemplative posture.

"Mom, which friends do you say hello to when you come to the park?"

"What do you mean?" I asked, turning to them. "You mean like the specific trees or flowers?"

"It could be anything," they said, shrugging. "Like today I am saying hello to the lampposts, the old ones with the little black squares on top. They stay in the ground but they look at everyone from the sky."

notes for themselves

FIERCENESS

(for my children: shapeshifters, creators, persons outside the binary)

What looks and sounds fierce might be more or less soft, loud, short, tall, or fluid than what we were raised to understand.

Writer Ocean Vuong speaks of growing up around boys who used the language of violence and conquest to boast of their relationships. "I bagged her," "I got her." Perhaps fierceness is about counteracting the possession of bodies, thoughts, and activities assumed by others. It is about claiming or reclaiming a right, purpose, or ownership. This could be power, money, space, or a clear pathway to being heard.

The Italian violinist Nadja Salerno-Sonnenberg, one of my childhood idols, performed Tchaikovsky's Violin Concerto with the Aspen Chamber Orchestra in the summer of 2000. During rehearsals she was two to four steps ahead of us at all times, not just artistically but also in speed. She made each musical gesture with the aim of defying expectations, perhaps even her own. She was also testing reflexes; in order to follow her we had to sit on the edge of our seats, bypass looking at the conductor, anticipate her every move. The concert was even wilder than the rehearsals. At certain points she turned around, smiled a devious grin, and headed off in a brisker tempo.

Perhaps unsurprising is the criticism she received, particularly at the height of her career, for the way she dressed for performances—pantsuits with an unusually low-cut neckline—and her expressive faces onstage. Critics and audience members described her looks while playing as "unappealing," her smiles as "grimaces." They were unprepared for a fiery, demanding leader who never made a minute for apologies. And who held nothing back. I wonder if people would have criticized her clothing and facial mannerisms if she were a man.

How is fierceness cultivated? What makes our bodies fierce?

Comments from colleagues and audience members about my "gentle" leadership style as the first violinist of a string quartet— could there be more incisive energy from you(?), but actually, not too much because it's uncomfortable to watch—were maddening. So were mixed compliments about how my way of moving when I play is so non-ego-driven, so feminine.

An older man once pushed me to have a long conversation with him after a workshop I ran on communication. He needed to tell me how my posture onstage was not working for me. After listening politely, I mentioned my long-time work with the Alexander Technique and how I took issues of posture seriously in my own life and with students. But he was not interested; he was consumed by all that he noticed.

How long will we wait for an older set of assumptions to catch up, to confront those who can only see cisgender heterosexual men as legitimate leaders? Can gender, its fluidity and new definitions, heal and excite us instead of making divisions?

And what about our softness. Our vulnerability, our lightness of touch, our relinquishing of control, our uninterrupted listening. Perhaps these can be reframed as our fiercest expressions.

We want to know when we're being treated well or dishonorably. Can we speak up, keep an edge? Fierceness followed swiftly by truth, and joy.

donors, poachers, and the creative aura

"Where do you make things?" a man asked my child. My child was dressed in an all-black ensemble with purple lipstick, waiting in a line with four other young people to receive an award for a piece of music they had written.

He tried again, "Do you work at your desk, or do you have another place at home for writing?"

It was an innocent question, but I could tell who he was right away.

I stepped forward to intervene right as my child raised their eyes to give the man a disaffected glance. "In my room," they responded in a monotone voice, turning their body to face the next young person in line. They seemed to have it covered.

The man was around sixty and had a lined face. He wore a jacket and a bow tie and looked like he could be somebody's grandfather. He also appeared a bit too eager, hunkering in closely to the five young people. Only parents and program coordinators should have been standing there. The hallway was crowded, and he didn't seem to fit in. I looked around for the directorial assistant assigned to us—she was out of view.

As we stood in line, I stared ahead at the man, wondering what he was thinking. Perhaps he just wanted tips, hints into this world from younger people who seemed to be on the right path. This couldn't be too harmful.

But as I saw him walk forward to a different young person and tap them on the shoulder with the same excessive enthusiasm, I knew what was happening.

Another parent in the hallway moved in and we exchanged a look. Even though our children were acquainted with this scenario, they still needed a hand.

We stood closer together to shield them from outsiders. This man would not get anything from these children today. I was protective of my child and of all of these children who were being celebrated for their creative output. I wanted to smother the gleam in this man's eyes. Don't prey on our children's creativity, I thought, my frustration rising up. Stop poaching.

———

History is full of the intertwined relationships between artists and their admirers. An artist emerges with meaningful work, and audiences rush to become fans. News spreads about this artist's talent, and suddenly there is standing room only at their events; they can barely produce fast enough. Or, more likely, an artist makes work for fifty years before it starts to be recognized. In both cases the artists' friends and admirers help to move their careers forward, even funding projects and commissioning artwork.

In many disciplines, artists prior to the early 19th century owed their livelihoods to courts, churches, and distinguished individuals. It was a job—J. S. Bach, for example, was expected to write at least one large new work for his church musicians every week—but also a kind of tethered creativity. The artist needed the money to live and work, and the institution or sponsoring nobleperson provided. The artist's power lay in their ability to create. Looking at this arrangement from a more modern perspective, the artist could be viewed as the more vulnerable party, at the mercy of whomever held the funds. At the time, however, someone like Bach probably didn't see a disadvantage to his situation; he was content to write sacred music with predictable regularity.

Since artists today, especially in the United States, still require funding to make art/produce a recording/rent a space, we reenact the centuries-old solicitation. We raise money by appealing to individuals with whom we have a personal relationship and who connect with our art-making. We recognize donors by giving them ownership of some of the final artistic product: a mention in a CD booklet, a name on a building, a private event in our studios. We accept commissions from donors who make requests of us—asking for a piece to be written for four cellos, or specifying a particular structure, tone, or subject for a painting—and we try to negotiate terms that don't compromise our artistic freedom.

While I was a fellowship student at the Aspen Music Festival in Colorado in the 1990s and early 2000s, I engaged with many wealthy individuals who supported student musicians. We attended dinners for artists and their sponsors at extravagant residences with multiple adjacent buildings, pools, and lawns against the backdrop of the Rocky Mountains. Sometimes we played concerts in houses with living rooms the size of small concert halls. In one home, built and owned by an inventor ahead of his time, even the doors and cabinets were operated with switches like those for lights.

We were treated to catered brunches and three-course dinners. Risotto three ways; local meats and fishes cooked on outdoor grills; a cake station. Donors went out of their way to make us feel included in their lives for the summer, inviting us and our friends to their other mountain homes. Having grown up in an average middle-class household, I was amazed by the donors' ease of life and the prevalence of staff who cooked and cleaned. Homes for two people had four to six bathrooms.

As welcoming as the donors were, my friends and I often felt scrutinized as if members of a rare species. The chasm between us and them seemed immense, and it wasn't just age and socio-economic level—it was also how differently we spent our days. A donor would start asking questions and had no interest in stopping. "Where did you grow up?" "Tell us about your schooling and how many hours you practice the piano every day." "You lived in Boston, right, so did you go to a pre-college program?" Some wanted to be attached by association to our names and institutions and the people we worked with. They wanted to "discover" us. I found it overwhelming to be questioned in large groups. The room would go quiet as musicians took turns talking about our upbringings, studies, and daily routines. We were on display.

Female friends of mine were apprehensive about spending too much time with male donors who felt entitled to time with the artists they were supporting. After dinner a charismatic man might corner two younger female artists. "Do you have siblings?" "Really, so many sisters!" "Interesting that your mother is a painter—you should visit the gallery I support in Chicago during the year. I could give you a private tour." We were constantly on the lookout for our friends. If an older man or woman started latching onto a younger musician, a few of us would interrupt their conversation. "Hey, come over here, look at the view from the balcony!"

One never quite knew what a donor's intentions were, especially with younger performers in whom they might have had a particular interest.

Driving back to our dorms and apartments on the curvy mountain roads after dinner, we debriefed about the people we met. While all of the people in the room were genuinely kind, one or two showed the tell-tale looks of poachers. In staking out our youth and artistry, a poacher could be identified by their body language—stiff in their posture with focused eyes, looking like they were at work. They would survey the room, checking out young artists they heard perform recently or who already had a budding career. Then they would approach with determination. In contrast, other donors appeared physically relaxed, draped over chairs with a glass of wine and enjoying the company of the musicians. These donors didn't express the same level of need to be with us.

———

To clarify, occasionally a donor is a poacher, but a poacher can be anyone. They can be young and old and in between. Donors have financial means and are committed to helping artists, but poachers may or may not be in a situation to help an artist monetarily.

The act of creativity poaching involves someone (such as a donor) trying to extract a creative aura of sorts from an artist, to possess some of the artistic process itself. Creativity poaching is not a stealing of artwork or intellectual property; it is a preoccupation with artistic energy and talent.

Poachers find artists whose work engages them, and they become infatuated. In this vulnerable state their guard is down, which makes an artist's guard go up. Poachers meet artists at concerts, galleries, openings, book talks, online, at home—anywhere an artist's work is shown. Their interest can be reflective of the fanaticism present in the artistic process itself.

My child had recently encountered two women like this at a family wedding. The two heard my child perform, had thoughts for "this remarkable young artist," and wanted alone time with them. "You have a real gift. You know you're special, right? Not everyone can do what you do—not everyone knows what you know." In our child's performance the women experienced something they didn't have, and they wanted to own it.

The poacher/artist relationship requires boundaries similar to the donor/artist relationship, but these can be hard to set. Often the poachers swoop in when musicians are on a post-concert high; their intensity seems to peak when musicians want to start winding down. One man approached me in the lobby after a string quartet concert, eyes glittering, smile wide across his face. He had a full head of black hair and wore a gray suit with a yellow and purple striped tie. "What extraordinary artistry," he said, leaning in. "I haven't seen playing with that kind of poetry since the Cleveland Quartet came through here in the late 80s. Will you be coming to the reception later? I want to show you a book, and I have questions for you. Please accept this note." He handed me a handwritten card about my quartet's Beethoven interpretation and exited the lobby.

My colleague agreed that the man was probably harmless, but he offered to stay with me at the reception in case it got weird. We arrived to a packed house and tried for thirty minutes to get to the buffet table while standing shoulder-to-shoulder with audience members; after playing two hours of quartet music, all we wanted to do was eat. When we finally got to the cheese station, the man was waiting for us with his wide smile and a book about violin maker Antonio Stradivari. People mentioned that he was the chamber music series' biggest supporter and liked to talk to first violinists of string quartets.

Every time we tried to end the conversation, he continued. "I noticed that all of you move side-to-side rather than up and down. And you, in particular, tend to look upwards as you cue—what do you imagine as you lift the scroll of your violin?" "Do you still play solo recitals even though you're in a full-time group?" "Can you describe your different approaches to sound when playing a Beethoven quartet versus a solo piece by Paganini?"

Shouldn't I have been glad that he received my performance with the kind of scrutiny to detail that I gave it myself? Isn't this the kind of conversation that I wanted to have after a performance? I did my best to answer the man's questions, balancing patience for his interest in my musical approach and annoyance at his close-talking. Every time I spoke he seemed to be collecting my responses, storing them away in a mental vault, perhaps to compare later with other first violinists' answers. But couldn't I have endured this mild discomfort for the sake of his curiosity? After the party my colleague and I identified what made this man a poacher: his questioning had gone beyond what I had experienced before from string quartet fans—it was an attempt at acquisition.

Artists experience versions of poaching all the time from within our industry. Managers lurk at competitions and award ceremonies to seek out new talent to represent; composers try to coerce performers to play their music (and conversely, performers try to convince composers to write them a piece over another performer); publishers fight over access to an artist and their newest work. Many of these scenarios are unpleasant, even if they are part of the trade. When is it ok to treat artists and artistic work like commodities, without regard for the artist's humanity? Do we artists endure it when the poacher has something to give in return?

———⌒᠀

I think about how obsessive artists can be, with our fixated working habits and needing to get things just right. We record a ten-second passage of music 200 times to play the phrasing the way we hear in our heads, then we spend hours agonizing over it; we revise a four-word passage for three weeks, then decide it needs to be six words instead. We also study each other's sounds and methods the way we collect objects and thoughts. I am inordinately excited when someone I admire publishes a new book, shares a series of paintings, or releases a recording. I stay up late watching performance videos and reading new poetry, inspired by the ease and poignancy of others' work. All artists I know get a little obsessed a lot of the time.

Strangely, in this way, a curious artist's energy is not so different from a poacher's energy. It is like a crush that becomes compulsive to the point of combustion. Those entire-body crushes that heat up a sidewalk when you catch a glimpse of "that person" on the street. You would do anything just to catch a whiff of their essence. The poaching crush, however, seems to be on the creative spirit itself, or at least on the air around it, and whoever holds it. I wonder how protective creators need to be of this kind of creative vapor. Should they maintain some kind of physical distance because of it, or is that a myth?

I saw a well-known young composer I'd met once coming out of an elevator at a building in New York's Lincoln Center. She was wearing an expression of trepidation as she looked both ways before stepping out. I was on my computer close to the elevator, waiting for my child to finish an after-school program. I imagine the composer was checking to see who was there; she must need to guard herself against classical music fans when she's in that kind of environment. I waved to her, and her facial expression lightened as she walked over to say hello. I thought I posed no threat, but as she left to find her room I wondered if for a moment I had become one of her too-eager fans.

On a ferry trip out to an island I saw someone who looked like John Corigliano, another composer of an older generation. Corigliano has such a distinctive face that I felt almost certain it was him, but I had to make sure. Even in the middle of the ocean he was surrounded by five or six people in their twenties—possibly students. There was patchy cell phone service, so I waited half the ferry ride to confirm that it was indeed Corigliano, heading to be composer-in-residence at an island music festival. So much went into recognizing a man who either longed to be free of his niche fame or loved the attention while away from New York City.

I debated whether or not it would be for my sake or for his to push through the ferry traffic to reintroduce myself, twenty years after meeting him at Juilliard. In this remote location, would he have welcomed the recognition or needed a break from obsequious people? Would he care that I enjoy teaching his violin and piano sonata? As the ferry docked at the island port, I watched Corigliano gather his things and walk to the lower level, escorted by the young composers. Our profession is all about personal connections, but in the end, I decided (perhaps wrongly, I don't know) not to say hello.

If what philosopher Walter Benjamin said is true—a collector comes alive in a book rather than the book coming alive in the collector—perhaps the fiercest creativity poachers are afraid of losing themselves. And I understand: we all fear that we will become invisible, that we will fade away. Holding onto things and people seems like the only option when faced with chaos and death. The constant striving and possibility for growth inherent in a creative life is one of the reasons I choose to spend my time in this way. Otherwise my neuroticism, my fanaticism, my obsession with minutiae would be paralyzing. But in seizing what we deem to be special, we gain nothing from art's freedom. We lose ourselves all over again.

Cummington

"Sorry I'm early," says a man's cheery voice, announcing his entrance into the building. A woman's voice responds, after a laugh, "An apology isn't necessary, and it's a good thing you're here!" The man chuckles in the back of his throat and I hear the creak of the stairs as he heads up to the second floor of the Cummington Community House for a meeting. I cannot see the woman in the other large room, but from her authoritative tone on the phone she seems to be a town official. She arrived after I was already working at the round table in the public space opposite hers.

The tack board in the Community House entryway is crowded with paper: listings for crop shares and book clubs, town committee notes from the year, and brochures about Fiber Optics coming to the region. I know it is inevitable, but I have trouble imagining this area of western Massachusetts with reliable high-speed internet. In years past the Old Cummington Creamery, Cummington's general store, was one of the only places for miles to host Wi-Fi in a public space. One time when it was down, I asked an employee when it would be fixed. She shrugged and declared to me with a mixture of irritation and nonchalance, "There is nothing we can do about it right now." Her delivery implied: what could you possibly need in the rest of the world that you can't find in Cummington?

Around 12:15 I exit the Community House and begin my almost two-mile walk up to lunch. I see a woman who looks familiar walking on the other side of Main Street; we wave to each other. In the five weeks I spend each summer in this town of 900 people, I cross paths with dozens of Cummington residents at the Creamery and at the Village Church. There is a good chance this woman and I have seen each other several times before.

I turn around for a moment to survey Cummington's half-mile-long Main Street. What a stunning portrait of a western Massachusetts hamlet in summer: orange and yellow flowers blooming in yards; homes lining the streets; plentiful leaves on trees waving like feathers in the July breeze. I stand in the middle of the street and see no cars—no one even turns down the road from Route 9. I think about the 1945 film *The Cummington Story* and how little the town has changed in the past seventy-five years since its filming. Although the film is shot in black-and-white, on first glance the homes and town scenes are almost identical now to how they appeared then. What has changed in Cummington, and what has remained?

———~♂

"The strangeness between people breaks down when they live and work and meet together as neighbors," says Reverend Carl Sangree, the minister of one of the Cummington churches, and the narrator of *The Cummington Story*. At the beginning of the film we see a bus stopping on Main Street and a few people with suitcases getting off. Right away Sangree tells us that the newcomers are European refugees, and that he is helping them to acclimate to small-town society. The refugee families set up their lives in a large home on Main Street; strangers are seen greeting each other in the street; refugees sit next to Cummingtonites in Sangree's church.

We also see hints that some townspeople are not universally pleased with the refugees' arrival. The woman at the general store stares hard at the man called "Joseph" when he first comes in. She sells him whatever items he needs, but she looks at him with distrust. By the end of the film, however, we feel good about the welcome the Europeans receive in Cummington. Refugees and townspeople play music together, and Cummington men invite Joseph to whittle wood with them around the stove. At the end of the film, Joseph is said to return to his home in Europe, presumably content to bring home his experiences from America.

It is easy to believe, if one does not know Cummington, that the people in the film are actors, that the town is created as a set for an idyllic New England community. The film showcases adults socializing and farming, and children walking to school through the fall leaves. The scenery suggests an impossibility—does this fabled town with charming homes and two large churches really exist? Do we believe, by the end of the film, that Cummington would openly welcome a host of refugees entering their community—is it propaganda, or reality? And perhaps a larger question: can outsiders truly become insiders in a small town?

When I first watched *The Cummington Story* I was struck by how beautifully the film portrayed a town that I love, heightened by the American-pastoral film score written by composer Aaron Copland. But I was also curious about the film's aim. It seemed to address small-town conservatism but not wrestle with it; the film ends pleasantly. The film could have been an advertisement for what I knew of stereotypically quiet New England ways: Come to our town—we might be suspicious of you, but we'll take you in and we'll grow to like you, we promise! There had to be more to the film's story.

What I discovered was that it was one of twenty-six short films made by the United States Office of War Information (OWI) in the mid-1940s, designed to offer perspectives on American life to its allies during World War II. Some of the films were comical, like the ten-minute "Autobiography of a Jeep," but many were poignant propagandist films about American life. *The Cummington Story* was part of a smaller, more specific set of fourteen films showing "The American Scene," designed to give a window into life in New England, the Midwest, the Northwest, and the South.

Back in the late 1930s, the OWI's Bureau of Motion Pictures (BMP) division became involved in screening any Hollywood films for portrayals of Americans in war. The liberal directors of the BMP wrote a manual in 1942 detailing its anti-fascist stance, vowing to remove or rephrase anything that smelled of what the OWI viewed as fascism in Hollywood. "Any form of racial discrimination or religious intolerance, special privileges of any citizen are manifestations of Fascism, and should be exposed as such," the manual read. It was in this climate that the OWI took on its own production of short propaganda films to send specific messages about America and the country's intentions in wartime. Cummington's embrace of European refugees—mostly Jewish people fleeing Nazi oppression, although their history is never explicitly mentioned in the film—fit into a larger message of American kindness and tolerance.

—⁓୭

"Cummington has historically acted as a safe haven," said Carla Ness, a realtor, longtime resident of the Cummington area, and one of the town's historical commissioners. She and I met on a cold and wet early October afternoon in 2019 as the leaves were at the height of their autumnal glory. I had requested a tour of Cummington's Kingman Tavern Museum, and since the museum was not open regularly during the fall and winter months, Ness offered to give me a private tour of the space's historical arts and objects. She explained that while Cummington's population has always been small—the town was its largest in size, 1,200 people, in 1830—it has also had an unusual penchant for taking in those who seek shelter.

Reverend Sangree brought forty-four mostly Jewish refugees to Cummington during World War II. They stayed in his red house on Main Street that also functioned as the town hostel. A century earlier, in the mid-1800s, Cummington was home to abolitionists who hid enslaved people in the town's homes and barns as part of the Underground Railroad. According to the Cummington Historical Commission, a significant number of townspeople were vocal opponents of slavery in the decades preceding the Civil War. One named Hiram Brown and his family were excommunicated from Cummington's Village Congregational Society in the 1850s because of Brown's radical anti-slavery perspective, specifically his criticism of the church for not doing more to condemn slavery.

Perhaps it was the small size of Cummington and the close living quarters that forced community. Perhaps too it was the history of what we would now call progressive ideals, epitomized through Sangree's actions, that helped the visitors find refuge. A small Massachusetts town also found influence with the American Transcendentalist movement, whose key players were guests in

Cummington at William Cullen Bryant's home. This poet and editor of the *New York Evening Post* for fifty years was born and raised in Cummington and later spent summers there from 1865 until his death in 1878. Writers like Ralph Waldo Emerson and Henry David Thoreau were known to gather at his homestead to discuss scholarship, the rights of Native Peoples to land, and anti-slavery stances. Transcendentalists also celebrated the solace of the natural world.

The Office of War Information could have made one of its fourteen "The American Scene" films about any one of the infinite picturesque towns in New England. Did the makers of *The Cummington Story* even know of Cummington's history of humanitarian efforts, and how unusual Cummington's actions were overall?

Sangree's own progressive efforts were the catalyst behind the refugee project. He reached out through the General Council of Congregational Christian Churches to bring Europeans to Cummington. It was also he who invited an old friend—Howard Southgate Smith, the screenwriter working on the OWI short films—to visit him in Cummington. The screenwriter was on his way up to Maine to look at settings for the final film in the "American Scene" series, and he was so interested in Cummington's refugee hostel that he never went farther north.

I am putting together pieces of the story. Cummington was a town that would not have applied to be showcased, but, when discovered, turned out to be a model subject for the propagandist film. The townspeople were frustrated with Reverend Sangree's opportunism, but they enjoyed the attention of having a film crew in the town for two months. In the film's honest portrayals of real townspeople, one can feel Cummington's unique magnetism.

I turn onto Harlow Road for the final ascent up to camp, following the hand-painted sign in the shape of an arrow that reads "Greenwood." The sign points in the general direction of the camp, but its haphazard quality both lacks authority and evokes gentleness. Insects buzz around my perspiring head as I draw more frequent breaths on the steep incline. I am careful not to lose my footing on the gravel road, which has caused many flat tires. On one evening a flock of wild turkeys chased me back down the hill before taking flight up into the trees.

I am almost too far away to hear sounds from camp, but I know I will be greeted as I approach by a string quartet fervently rehearsing music by composer Felix Mendelssohn in the practice cabin called "Villa-Lobos," named after composer Heitor Villa-Lobos. That cabin, one of Greenwood's oldest, sits closest to Harlow Road and was built by campers and faculty in the 1940s. I can hear faint strains coming from a single oboe. The instrument sounds like a distant, delicate reed flute, a mesmerizing voice in the hot July sun.

My own pull to Cummington is through Greenwood Music Camp, an intensive musical experience for teenagers in a natural environment, fertile for personal and artistic growth and development. As a camper at Greenwood in the 1980s and 90s I made the best friends of my life, ran around in bare feet, and played string quartets all day. I also felt free and welcomed for who I was. Founded in 1933 by progressive musicians and educators Bunny (Dorothy Fay) and Dwight Little and Ruth (Hill) MacGregor, the camp relocated to an eighty-acre farm in Cummington in 1940. I went to Greenwood for many summers, and my experiences there became increasingly more layered and meaningful.

When I was fourteen I kept up a regular correspondence with another Greenwood camper during the year, exchanging eleven-page letters about twice a month. The real world felt like too much to bear after five weeks of playing chamber music in bare feet, so we kept it alive through longing in handwritten form. At the height of missing Greenwood, I wrote my friend a prose poem set in a fantastical world in which the inhabitants of the town were so telepathically connected to one another that they had no need for speech. Greenwood relationships involved such special bonds—perhaps these could be transformed into a new kind of communication. At times we compared Cummington to the fictional town of Brigadoon in the Scotland highlands, only perceptible to outsiders one day every 100 years. Otherwise the town was unattainable, shrouded in the highland mist.

In my third summer at Senior Camp, a viola teacher surprised me one day by saying that I would be playing some viola that week. I was already a committed violinist and felt worried about making time for another instrument. But I borrowed a spare viola for the afternoon and sat on my bed, plucking out notes and trying to read music written in alto clef. The next afternoon the teacher put Elliott Carter's *Elegy* for viola and piano on the music stand in front of me.

"I'm not good enough to play a piece like that on the viola," I said.

"Sure you are, just play the first line." He pointed to the music.

I looked at the notes and stumbled through them. I played the first line.

"Ok, now play it again, but play it *gray*."

"What do you mean?" I asked. This was all going too quickly; my mind was in overdrive. I already felt like I was trying to learn key points of a foreign language in mere hours.

"You have an entire world of sounds and colors in front of you," he said. "But right now, you play with only one kind of sound. Use your imagination, try it."

I played the first line: gray.

"Good, now play it red."

I played the music: red.

Then purple, then white, then green. I could not believe how much I could change my sound simply by stimulating my imagination. The dramatic change had taken no practicing, only a shift in intention and willingness.

That evening I played violin in a masterclass for a guest artist, and everything sounded dull. Like the world was cast in black and white, or just gray. The next day I lay on the ground under a tree for an hour, gazing at the "Greenwood Blue," the vibrant color that appears when blue sky peeks through green leaves. My artistic perspective was forever changed, and I was determined to make my playing correspond to the colorful world around me.

William Cullen Bryant wrote about this same sky a century earlier, after multiple visits to Cummington. In "Lines on Revisiting the Country," he mused about his home landscape.

> I stand upon my native hills again,
> Broad, round, and green, that in the summer sky,
> With garniture of waving grass and grain,
> Orchards, and beechen forests, basking lie.

Cummington was for him, as it was for other writers, artists, and musicians who found their way to the small town through the Cummington School for the Arts, for the Greenwood campers, for the World War II refugees, a getaway from life elsewhere.

Here I have 'scaped the city's stifling heat,
Its horrid sounds, and its polluted air.

The man called "Joseph" in *The Cummington Story* was played by
Werner Königsberger, an Austrian refugee brought to Cummington by Rev. Sangree. Although in the film Joseph goes back to
Europe, Königsberger and his wife Alice became residents of Cummington. Their family was one of those I heard about on my tour
of the Kingman Tavern Museum, who found a prosperous life in
America. Perhaps the makers of the film underestimated the determination of refugees like the Königsbergers; also, they did not fully
understand the power of the western Massachusetts hills to draw
people in.

——————

In present times Cummington and Greenwood could be viewed
as a kind of utopia. Together they share an idyllic, secluded landscape. Both communities meet in the summer when Greenwood
campers sing with townspeople at Cummington's Village Church.
Greenwood is a word-of-mouth organization and has never adver-
tised; it relies on its stellar reputation and strong alumni base
for applications and support. Campers stay for years, and family
members with musical interest tend to be involved with the camp
for generations. The Senior Camp has had only two directors in
ninety years, the Junior Camp only three.

Given Cummington's size and contentedness in particular, it
would be easy for this community to bask in its charming small-
town-ness, to not seek outside perspectives. Even though the com-
punction of people like Rev. Sangree, Hiram Brown, and others is
part of Cummington's energetic stamp, the woman at the Cream-

ery's apparent disinterest in the outside world represents one aspect of town sentiment.

Any utopian community has the potential to set up false promises of perfection, which can come at a cruel price (i.e., religious cults that fail to deliver whatever salvation or immunity they were promising their members). In other cases, so-called utopias hold on to times of past glory, becoming tired and unfocused in the process. Nostalgia can inhibit a community's ability to see itself clearly. When I returned to Greenwood in 2006 to teach on the faculty I worried about the strength of my own nostalgia. I was initially ecstatic about the camp's long commitment to the coexistence of artistic and community values—what transpires at Greenwood is the result of the three essential elements originally defined by founder Bunny Little: "the best food, place, and music." The first year, however, I indulged in my memories, perhaps sharing them too often with fellow faculty and campers. No place has touched my life the way Greenwood has, but I had to consciously stay above the temptation to live in the past.

While nostalgia in the form of tradition fuels part of Greenwood's magic (as it does for many summer camps), it is also recognized by many community members as potentially limiting; if improvements aren't made to the camp and new musical voices aren't introduced, the personal and artistic environment cannot grow. I would like to think that the steadiness of Greenwood and Cummington's aims and work helps both communities from falling into false idealism.

———

When almost at Greenwood I see the quartet from the Villa-Lobos practice cabin making their way to lunch. They hop quickly over large stones on the gravel road, carrying instruments on their backs—eccentric creatures dancing in bare feet. The oboist has already departed from her cabin across the road. I hear only wind through the trees and the murmur of a lawn mower.

I check the mailbox at the top of the hill before going into Greenwood's campus. Several letters lie inside, one marked for me: Becca Fischer, Greenwood Music Camp, Cummington, MA 01026. I open the letter as I walk to the dining hall. It is from the former director of Junior Camp, saying hello and thanking my young child for finding a watch that she lost on her last visit. Our generations coincide. I remember playing my first Greenwood audition in that director's living room at the age of ten.

As I walk through the grassy clover toward the robust sound of voices and clinking silverware, I feel a call to immense service and responsibility. I see a new era unfolding. Who will become part of Greenwood in its next ninety years, part of Cummington in its next fifty? As we embrace new generations and voices, what, together, will we learn? Who else will call this land home?

> And, where the season's milder fervors beat,
> And gales, that sweep the forest borders, bear
> The song of bird, and sound of running stream
> Am come awhile to wander and to dream.
>
> —William Cullen Bryant (Cummington, MA)

notes for themselves

STILLNESS

(for my children: shapeshifters, creators, persons outside the binary)

When was it that I first heard stillness is a virtue, and discovered it was something I couldn't find? Stillness was associated with shame about doing too much.

"Why can't you stop thinking?" an exasperated violin teacher asked after watching me tie myself up in knots trying to execute a bowing technique. "You're constantly rushing the tempo, too. Maybe you should smoke weed or something. It would probably loosen you up, get you to calm down." I stood facing the teacher in the lesson, shifting my feet. "Uh," I said. "I'll try it again."

As a child my legs crawled with energy most days—the only way I could release it was to head outside and go. Long walks, dancing on sidewalks and streets, sometimes sports. After long car trips I would set up a workout area at our hotel stop for the night. While my family members brushed teeth in the small bathroom, I danced and ran in place, monitoring my body in the mirror to see how much of it I could move at one time. It also gave me a fighting chance at sleep.

When I grew older, bodily stillness seemed possible for me to achieve, but mental stillness, not so much. I was often told that my mind was too active: there was too much going on inside, which meant I must have something wrong with me. Often up early in the morning or up late at night, or both. I worked a lot, obsessed, talked to people (including myself), went outside.

The first time I went running I was dealing with depression, feeling tired and ruined most of the time, even though my mind couldn't stop racing. After walking to the running track one night after a long violin practice session, I ran a mile. Four times around the track winded me, but the exhaustion following the run was also electrifying. Maybe increased activity was the way to make it through.

Through a double-degree college program at two schools and in my 20s it was go-go-go. Work, run, work, run, work, run, play, work. My body started showing signs of fatigue in my early 30s. I experienced excruciating bouts of insomnia and was told that if I didn't find some way to slow down, my hormones would dry up and stop functioning altogether. I listened to these concerns; made time for cooking and eating warm lentils every day; took three-to-five-minute breaks between activities; practiced yoga and meditation; read before bed. I hoped that if I was quiet enough I might uncover new suppressed wisdom. But in meditation, with the loose purpose of noticing my breath, my mind was still focused on end goals. I added too many layers of thought to the puzzle of stillness. It was yet another pursuit.

Perhaps the idea of utility—applying myself in productive ways—could somehow direct me towards a less harmfully active life, or at least welcome a lower level of anxiety. Even though I knew the words *utility* and *production* marked me as yet another person substituting work for meaning, I couldn't help it. I felt aimless and insincere without a purpose that kept me doing things that "mattered."

A different violin teacher had addressed me thoughtfully in a lesson. "There is a lot going on inside of you," he said, "but that's ok—you can embrace these ideas." Together we identified the eight things that were clouding my brain, offering two more substantive ideas to occupy me instead. It wasn't exactly mental diversion, but more like positive replacement.

In the same way, I "used" my body during yoga while holding a still strength. Running made my active life too competitive, a doctor had told me, and I had to resist all of that. And yoga really did challenge me. For months at a time I sweated in the early morning or afternoon light, holding poses. But I couldn't keep up the practice, so I started running again.

In her essay "Peril," Toni Morrison reassures that stillness is a way of being creatively useful in times of oppression. That being still is keeping our heads down while we write and plan and craft— to overthrow regimes, to assert rights, to respond to chaos. Mental diversion? Actually, the opposite. Active (albeit quiet) purpose.

I struggle every day to embrace moments of stillness. They are just that—moments—not long, devoted hours. I smile at the beginning of a violin practice, breathe for a minute or two watching the city transition into night, catch my breath in front of a work of art. When a fragile self loses its tremble in the low light and is just, there.

Vinalhaven

a whim of erasure
opaqueness
knows how long
seafarers
have held terror

lost on deck
below
throbbing heads

waiting for
sun
on other side

must
remember
its way

2.

The town of Vinalhaven lies 15 miles off of midcoastal Maine and has an area of 168.69 square miles, but 86 percent of that area is water. The people who live on the island are 98 percent white, and their economies includes fishing, farming, and wind energy. You can take the ferry a few times a day to and from Rockland, but the last ferries leave at 4:30 p.m. from both terminals, so visitors can't forget the time—the motel options on the island are slim, and the bed and breakfast is often booked (or its owner decides not to open). The ratio of bothersome tourists to homeowners is low, and the town is pleased with that reality. Vinalhaven projects its self-sufficiency to the outside world: come for the day but then leave us alone.

3.

hurtling towards
unseen goals

hasty fog
moves through fir trees like
disparate ghosts

an open mouth
catches moisture
inhales
chilled burst of salt-water air candy

all things go
(thoughts, objects)
whatever is not fixed

4.

My small family is not the only group of people to try to hold Vinalhaven island as its own. Many come to embody another kind of time.

The man standing close to us in the ferry line is tall and slender. He is maybe sixty-five but he bounces in his sneakers like a seven-year-old. Amongst the man's many oddly shaped belongings I see he has a brown, rectangular stringed instrument case with frayed fabric on the corners.

5.

where riggings slap
violently against
masts
deafeningly
asynchronous

harbors hold tolls
passages sought
waiting
for inevitable gales

6.

"Do you have two violins in there, or is that a violin/viola case?" I ask.

The man, with fast glee, his first-grade energy almost gobbling up the words: "Oh, it's a violin/viola case, I'm playing a wedding on the island."

On board he plays us a few tunes. He hands me the violin.

We toss music back and forth as the ferry begins its slow movement through the harbor, gaining speed as it heads out to sea. A noiseless coastal rain starts to fall. The violin catches a few drops so I quickly put it away in the case's maroon velvet pouch, still soft but thin from use, wiping off the instrument with a cloth.

I try to say thank you to the man, to catch his attention before heading downstairs to join my family. But he is transfixed, his once jittery feet pacified by the music. He hums as he plays the melancholic viola, looking out to sea through the speckled rain.

7.

post office
grocery line-up
bank
B&B Airbnb
sandwich-slash-fish-eatery-slash-ice-cream-shop
Star of Hope
(late artist Robert Indiana's outsized
dilapidated
Victorian
home
campy American flags
boarded windows
pigeons enter the roof's hole)
motel
two souvenirs

"For Lobster Sales Order at the Gas Pump"

8.

The first vehicle contains an older man in a slow-moving truck who raises his hand in greeting. The next is a beat-up car full of twenty-somethings—the driver's hand doesn't leave the wheel, but she raises two fingers of hello.

Over and over this happens: one finger or two, a whole hand, sometimes the signal happens right at the very end, a split second before we pass. Is everyone waving as we drive by?

Hand gestures can be powerful, dangerous, comforting, and everything in between. The Vinalhaven car wave seems to be an innocuous show of kindness.

Do islanders shame those who don't participate? Some anonymity once and a while might be nice.

9.

a good day's work
sells out in 30 minutes
deep-sea diver hawking oysters
open trunk
swollen deft hands
shucked sensuous edibles
"The best around for sure"
a freelancer's eyes
reveal measured
peril

10.

On dark days and nights maybe this sign of human warmth is what saves those in a desperate situation. A code for a haven.

11.

erupting through impossibly
light
bright
green grass
nothing is ever quite still
doors open at night without children
(awake-dreaming
fear-murmuring)
rattling
senses a nerve
says BOO

12.

We ride in a rickety truck belonging to a man who runs several ad hoc businesses. Windows down, hair perpetually lifted with salty air.

He has promised to take us to a moss-covered forest. He is trying to get us to become islanders, to move into a different kind of life.

We pass the port and the swimming quarries. We pass homes either obscured by regal gates or covered precariously with blue tarps; porches are curated with colorful plants or littered with lobster traps.

He says he knows someone who is homebound and confined to a chair. The person is trying to sell their home because they need to move to the mainland for their health, but they can't do so without repairs—the floor is unstable, the wallpaper peels off in large sections. Without the cash to prepare their home or to leave the island they are stranded, in limbo.

13.

presented without distraction of human life
(only loons)
Cassiopeia
Orion and dippers
Milky Way's husky shimmer
underfoot
mucus
binds flesh to grass—
black slugs
with corrugated backs
multiply
in the yard before
dusk
island spirits
take form

14.

This place may be haunted—I swear it exerts a physical pull on my
frame. What more will it require of me?

15.

merciless cold
berates a still
pallid earth
unsure of footing
bitter breath
each held

alone
in the exacting darkness
white caps bring
euphoric brooding in
low light
twenty feet from
the sea

16.

Rapture (Entrückung): the final movement of Arnold Schoen-berg's *Second String Quartet.* A soprano sings, "I feel air of another planet . . . a tempestuous wind overwhelms me."

    The quartet plays eerie, cascading textures like fine nails swirl-ing over a chalkboard.

    The sentiments of foreignness, of feeling like an outsider, of engaging in the wonder of the earth. Overwhelmed and powerless, caught in the wind.

17.

an island cabin abandoned to rising water
summons adventurers
at low tide
(swim
cross land
bridge to cabin
summit)
Kevin Sean Mary
carved into walls

a profession of love
loose beer talk
main island portrait
from
glassless window
loyalty
test
(holding breath)
Vinalhaven
asks
will you stay close or
stray

18.

We sit watching the sea meet a vague horizon. The light is brought
forth in dense, salt-sharpened waves. We learn that the distinction
between grays and blues is either negligible or fierce. We wonder
how we could paint it, how it is spelled.

19.

caught mid-cry
between two granite
slabs not one
tooth amiss
above the raging
ocean its
alarming
fossilized

whiteness
perfectly preserved
a reminder
some things fall
captive just before
the waves

seeing in the world

(A DICTIONARY)

Quella (Italian: that)

Palermo, Sicily, 2001: Quella: noun, in the Italian language, feminine for "that." Italy is a country known for reinforcing gender stereotypes and, at times, for objectifying women (example: my fair-haired sister visited southern Italy wearing tank tops and shorts and was barraged by constant comments and whistles from men). Addressing a woman, or anyone, as quella seems offensive. Why not refer to her as la donna ("woman") or another appropriate title? What is the foreigner's role in questioning cultural practice?

My partner and I are visiting an island, but we feel in the center of things. We find hotel and hostel accommodations the day of. These are sometimes unlikely but charming locations like a basement with a moldy mattress in the resort town of Cefalù when all other places are booked, or a farm where the "vegetarian" pasta sauce is made with chunks of sausage. The farmer forces us to take jars of thick honey home to the States. My partner is fluent in Italian and delightful with people. I have let two years of college Italian slide.

In Palermo, we walk to a square to get sandwiches from a famous food cart—a local treasure, a destination eatery. Right after picking up the food, a police officer (carabinieri) in blue uniform strikes up a conversation with my partner. For now I am content not to try to follow their rapid, gestural banter. I sit down on a bench to eat the exquisite, roughly made sandwich with a huge slab of ricotta cheese and olive oil on a fresh roll. It is still warm—street food at its best.

My partner is holding pace with the Italian officer, laughing while simultaneously attempting to eat his enormous sandwich dripping with pieces of lamb meat. Lamb juice spills out of the sandwich paper onto the cobblestones in unavoidable trickles. I'm a bit annoyed that he is choosing to share our sandwich moment with the officer, but there is time; we are heading to eat cannolis afterwards. A woman's unrestrained laughter drifts across the busy square, a heartiness deep in her chest.

Finally, the officer leaves to patrol another area, bowing formally to me before he turns around. I nod in response.

My partner sits down, the front of his shirt now spattered lightly with meat grease. He pauses in thought, his mouth open in a question. With eyes looking upwards, he says slowly, "I didn't register this until now. I think right after that policeman said hello he asked me, 'E quella è la tua?'

'is *that* yours?'

talking about you . . ."

I take a moment to process. My cheap, tight-fitting summer clothes suddenly feel suffocating. The sun irritates my pale skin.

What am I, just a thing? The woman's laughter from across the square is now loud, grotesque.

————·~⁹

Maada'ookiiwin (Ojibwe: a gift for distribution)

Turtle Mountain Indian Reservation (land base for Turtle Mountain Band of Chippewa Indians, upon unceded Pembina Chippewa nation lands), North Dakota, USA, 2001: Maada'ookiiwin, noun, in the Ojibwe language, for "gift" or "gift for distribution." A gift can be both physical and experiential. Not everyone recognizes artistic work as a gift, whether it is a performance or a painting or a woven blanket. And not everyone wants or is open to receive an artistic experience. Perhaps the gift lies in the sharing between artists and communities, when there is no distinction between audience and performer.

————·~⁹

From my position onstage I can see the seats filling up with children, college students and adults. Several elders wearing traditional Native clothing enter the hall and welcome the orchestra musicians. My left hand moves silently over the strings, practicing passages from Claude Debussy's string quartet. I feel unsettled about transporting this orchestra, a European creation, to the reservation. What do I have to offer this community?

We are in North Dakota, but also in a place not of this state. I have been wondering about what past memories might layer this place, and what memories might have been excluded.

After our performance, the conductor of the Greater Grand Forks Symphony Orchestra addresses the crowd. His turtleneck and chinos accentuate his impressive height, as well as his large, gentle eyes.

"That Debussy really knocks me off my feet every time. Thank you to Turtle Mountain Community College for having us, and to the Chiara Quartet for starting off our program. We are excited to introduce the composer of the next piece, here from the Twin Cities to speak with our solo flutist about the work of bridging cultures."

Is the idea of bridging cultures presumptive? Can music ever really bridge what has happened in America? My mind drifts, anxiety rising, while the composer and flutist speak to the audience about their work together. I look down at the music and try to bring it into focus as the piece begins with a solo improvisation on Native American flute.

As I play with the orchestra and the flutist, I question my role. Music is my work, but I am searching to reframe the experience. I do not want to be in the position of bringing "good" music to a community that "needs" it. My nerves are rising and it's hard to engage. The orchestral work ends and all of us bow to applause from the audience. Suddenly one of the elders stands up and starts singing.

The man's voice fills the room more completely than the entire orchestra. He is expressing without restraint, and I am pulled in. A drum begins, beating in everyone's sternum bones.

Does this man's performance create a bridge? Everyone in the room stands up, honoring the gift.

———

L'image (French: image)

Paris, France, the Louvre, 1993: L'image, noun, in the French language, for "image," also "picture," "reflection." What we can grasp at any given time is a product of our exposure and openness. Travel is one of the most significant kinds of exposure; we are able to see ourselves, sometimes for the first time, through the lenses of culture and family, through the art we encounter.

———~୬

Years ago, I stand in front of the painting, my long, curly hair carrying a permanently frizzy halo from the March rain. *La Vierge aux rochers* (the *Virgin of the Rocks,* by Leonardo da Vinci) is a scene: four figures, two adults and two infants are surrounded by a rocky landscape. The two women, one woman in a red garment (angel) and another in darker fabric (Madonna), are caring for the babes. They appear otherworldly: their skin is smooth and creamy, their eyes uncreased, their expressions lifted and transcendent. They wear no halos, but their heavenly bearing is clear. The background is a cathedral-like forest with dark, black-green hues—it creates serenity but also distance and awe.

Walking alone through the galleries, taking notes on paintings in my small red notebook, I feel intoxicated by the freedom. I shuffle between artwork, acting like other tourists, politely whispering "pardon, je m'excuse." This solo expedition to the Louvre is a much-needed break from my parents, sister, and grandmother, all on vacation together. Despite my recently removed braces, I am consumed by internal voices questioning my worth, ridiculing my outfits.

The longer I stare at the painting the more I love these women. Maybe this ethereal family would accept me without question.

Suddenly a heavy man wearing shorts and a t-shirt enters the gallery.

"I think that's the one," he yells behind him. "Y'all move to the side. Get in the photo now, let's do this!"

The man pushes everyone, including me, to his left or right in an effort to get to the painting. A young boy around age seven with his face scrunched up in a cry, and an older girl with red pigtails around age twelve, accompany their father. Their mother follows, wearing 90s capri pants and a large t-shirt.

She walks up to the Da Vinci painting and almost tries to touch it.

"Hold on, this isn't the real Leonardo? Damnit, we got the wrong painting. No *Mona Lisa*. Look at that weird baby right there!" She points to the infant depiction of John the Baptist and laughs with a bite.

"Ok take the damn picture!" she shouts to the girl with red pigtails.

The man yells "Shut up!" as his son continues to whimper.

The girl takes the photo with her disposable camera and her mother yells to the room, "Where's the real painting? I gotta get that on camera."

The family continues to fuss while leaving the gallery.

My face feels hot, singed with humiliation. As I look around the room, other tourists roll their eyes and sigh. I move closer to the artwork in an effort to protect it from further harm, peering at the handsome faces again. The figures can't have noticed the interruption. Could I find refuge in Leonardo's forest?

———✎

Supposition (French: assumption)

Sault Ste. Marie, Canada, post-concert reception, 2018: Supposition, noun, in the French language, for "assumption," also "guess" or "presumption." Assumptions can contain fear and distrust. Even if a negative assumption is warranted, mitigating the perception takes time. How many positive experiences does it take to alleviate fear towards an entire culture?

———⌒୨

My makeup is sweated-through and smeared, and my feet in heels are in pain after a long concert. At least my shiny purple, floor-length gown hides my awkward and constantly shifting stance.

An older man and woman eye me from across the room. They look away as swiftly as possible when they see me turn my gaze towards them. Something feels off. To approach the couple, I extricate myself from an interminable conversation with a middle-aged man spraying red wine through his teeth.

Up close, the older man's eyes look watery. He speaks in a quavering voice. "It's wonderful that they renovated this old paper mill. Imagine—the machines used to reach thirty feet into the air!" He gestures upwards slowly with his right hand.

The petite older woman with bright green eyes and perfectly bowl-shaped silver hair nods her head in agreement.

The couple seems to be holding something back. Is my bright lipstick all over my teeth again? I should take off my heels to avoid towering over them. The circulation in my feet is being cut off anyways.

"We flew into the small Sault Ste. Marie airport in Michigan last night, and once we crossed the bridge into Canada, I could feel how much your city welcomes visitors." I am trying too hard.

"It's a lovely city," says the older woman. "But it's been a tough few days for us in the Canadian Sault Ste. Marie. Our economy is on the fence, you know." Her emerald eyes burn bright.

I realize it now: the couple is viewing me with fear. I will take the damn heels off.

"You mean . . . the tariffs?"

The woman looks nervously at her partner, her silver hair swaying. "Sault Ste. Marie is a leading steel manufacturing town here in Canada, and the States are our biggest customer. If the tariffs go into effect we can't possibly compete with cheaper labor and materials from overseas. Our town might not survive."

I stammer "I . . . I'm so sorry to hear that," finally stepping out of my heels.

The silver-haired woman lifts her eyebrows slightly at my three-inch loss of height, but she looks relieved. "Oh . . . good, well we didn't know which way you thought. Our friends in Michigan worship your president. They don't hear us anymore—we're like strangers to them."

I wish I could hug this couple. How can I show warmth, and solidarity? I round my shoulders inwards—maybe I will lose more height that way. The man puts his hands in his pockets in a kind of quiet defeat. His sad, half-closed eyes match his partner's pursed lips.

———

상 (Korean: figure)

Seoul, South Korea, Jogyesa Buddhist Temple, 2012: 상, noun, in the Korean language, for "figure," "statue," or "representation." How much of the meaning attributed to an inanimate figure is up to us? We feel a connection with a statue; we count on an object to remember. But can a physical object conjure the life of a community?

———

The temple gates are open twenty-four hours a day. It is the week of the Buddha's birthday, and even at this late hour couples are strolling, whispering, holding hands, laughing softly. Others sit and pray inside and outside of the dark-green temple containing three sixteen-foot-high golden statues of the Buddha.

Life feels wildly exuberant at 2:00 a.m., now that I have left my hotel and freed myself from the obligation to sleep. I walk under the colorful lanterns strung horizontally from tree branches—reds, yellows, oranges, blues, purples. They create a light tapestry swaying in the almost imperceptible breeze.

Earlier in the day a group of rowdy monks caught me by surprise. They ran through the streets wearing rough brown cloaks with hoods over their shaved heads, handing out laminated cards with a smiling, pink-cheeked Buddha on them. One man put his face close to mine, looking like he would holler with happiness. The group was naughty and conspiratorial, yet innocent and hilarious.

I stand outside of the temple, looking at the scene of public and private devotion. An older woman beckons from inside the temple for me to join her. She holds the arm of my jacket as I take off my shoes at the temple entrance, and she leads me to a mat.

The three Buddhas in front of me present identical expressions. Their golden bodies reflect the colorful flowers lying in offering at the statues' bases.

As I offer thanks for a stranger's welcome, worlds away, in every way, from the States, I check for the small, thin card still in my pocket. An energy similar to what the monks shared is pervasive: a community of unbridled, raucous elation, an uncommon way of expressive living.

I stay on the mat for a long time, but shorter than others around me. Both knees crack as I stand up and head over to put on my shoes. The night outside is shining.

———————

Chimurenga (Shona: revolution)

Harare, Zimbabwe, HIFA (Harare International Festival of the Arts), 2018: Chimurenga, in the Shona language, for "revolution." Photographers and portrait artists seek to capture the landscape of revolution in a single picture. Is it possible to portray the extremes of oppression, violence, inequality, unrest, including a release from all of the above? How would one paint the aftermath?

———————

The man in the photograph holds the Zimbabwean flag high in the air. He rejoices while he screams, his face caught in ecstasy bordering on rage. The people around him are also screaming, in mid-march. All of the artwork is defiant, including explicit anti-government rhetoric: "fuck the police."

I leave the exhibit at the National Gallery and sit on the front steps looking out at the buses—minivans with doors and seats removed to fit more standing people. They try to avoid craters in the pothole-ridden street.

At the Harare International Festival of the Arts for the second year in a row, I spend my days dipping into tents to hear music from Africa, Europe, and Asia. I walk through the art fairs and feel the American classical music bubble melting away.

Henry, my HIFA acquaintance from last year, waves from the other side of the street. He runs in between cars while crossing, his orange and black guard uniform a sharp contrast to the gray concrete. He sits down next to me on the museum steps, catching his breath.

"Hi there," says Henry. "You look the same as last year. How are you? I've got more thoughts."

As I turn to smile at him I know he must see my apprehension.

"Henry, it's good to see you again! I'm thinking about the tone of the artwork this year at the National Gallery. Is there no more censorship from the government?"

Henry, with a grim chuckle, "There has always been censorship. But with thirty-six years of the Mugabe dictatorship over, regulating art isn't a priority. We ran through the streets for days—it was beautiful. You probably saw in the photographs." He raises a fist in the air. "We still don't have enough money, but it will come."

Last year's unemployment number for Zimbabwe, 99.1%, comes into my head. "Money is so divisive. In the States the richest people continue to get richer. I know you argued with me last year that our new president would bring more wealth to our country, but only the wealthiest seem to have benefited."

"You know how I feel about this," Henry says, while tossing a rock into the street. "We would have picked him too because he has the money."

"A lot of people in the States voted for him for the appearance of success. They thought he was going to save them from insecurity, but he only wants to be in government for the possibility of absolute power."

"Look, our leaders are terrible humans too, and they do nothing for us," says Henry with a shrug. "The police are so corrupt that they stop our cars all of the time asking for bribes. But we're ok—Zimbabweans are tough."

I nod, throwing a rock into the street. "I remember last year when HIFA reimbursed us in cash that was brown and taped together like wax paper. I hadn't seen $2 bills in many years."

"Real money is kind of like a ghost here. We all use e-cash and the banks hardly have any physical money. I'm surprised the festival gave it to you."

I rub my arms in the cool sun, uncomfortable. "How much hope is there for Zimbabwe? Will there be real change now that Mugabe is gone?"

"Who knows, but we're hoping. The police won't change—it's the way they are here. By the way, I forgot to mention last year: you know a lot about American politics. Why don't you run for office in the States?"

"I try to stay informed about US politics," I say, laughing. "But it's a dead end. I'm happy as a musician. Music brings me to places like this, where I can mind my own business and have these kinds of talks. But what about you? You seem to follow politics."

Henry, smiling broadly, "It's different here, but no, I also have no serious interest in politics. Just these kinds of talks too."

We watch the buses careen through the nearby intersection, zooming around the potholes.

notes for themselves

ENOUGH

(for my children: shapeshifters, creators, persons outside the binary)

Enough.

Maybe we have given up—we are done, over it, too much has already come to pass. Exhaustion resonates in this word—*enough*. Or maybe we have reached the natural end and relaxation ensues— let it go, it is good for now. Or we are affirming—this is enough, what I am doing in a day (year, hour, moment) is enough.

J. S. Bach's sublime Cantata 82, *Ich Habe Genug* ("I have enough" or "It is enough") wrestles textually and musically with this word. As the singer explains in the first Aria, a melancholic dance:

"I have enough,
I have taken the Savior, the hope of the righteous,
into my eager arms.
I have enough! I have beheld Him;
my faith has pressed Jesus to my heart;
now I wish, even today
with joy to depart from here."

A sigh of relief. A final release. According to the text, the author can now be content with death after holding "the Savior." Bach's otherwise churning music turns to a major key. The solo voice and oboe intertwine, a glimmer of elation in their exchange.

What is enough for us? Can we be simultaneously unsatisfied and at peace? Peace with where we are, with never ever quite being done?

New York City started to shut down the day before I performed *Ich Habe Genug* in March 2020 at Columbia University with Ensemble Baroklyn and pianist Simone Dinnerstein. There was a case of possible exposure to COVID-19 at Columbia, so the University acted quickly, suspending classes and closing their facilities to the outside. The musicians decided to continue with the performance, but instead of playing to a flesh-and-blood audience, we serenaded a set of high-quality mics and video cameras over livestream with no one else in the hall. A small ensemble of string players, a singer, and an oboist surrounded Dinnerstein at the piano. It was an intimate feeling onstage, like gathering in a living room.

As we played Bach's pastoral second Aria, "Schlummert ein" ("Fall asleep"), we shared the chilling uncertainty that none of us knew when we would play our next concert. "Fall asleep, you weary eyes, close softly and pleasantly!" The looks we gave each other had new meaning. We questioned—were we also done, and for how long? As everything dissolved, everything also started mattering.

In our nonstop capitalist culture, we are used to things being earned, even weekends and time and space. We may examine the worth of items and experiences, but without a structure for feeling fulfilled, we try to accumulate more. As the band Capital Cities sings, "I want it all and nothing less."

Bach's cantata challenges us to look deeper at how we measure contentment, as a matter of perspective. I may not be in the position to view death as a joy, for example, but the anonymous writer of the text (possibly a Christian martyr) is. Just as the author looks to find release from the world, perhaps in this current moment we try to disassociate from constant need, delivered to us as speedily as possible. Having or being enough could be an antidote to impatience and greed. Would we also sleep "softly and pleasantly" if we no longer felt the pressure of production and acquisition?

Zen Buddhist Norman Fischer writes that Zen practitioners are "really very materialistic." They appreciate all things, "time and space flowing endlessly by, we ourselves flowing endlessly by." Fischer is describing the result of practicing gratitude—in recognizing everything that exists, practitioners become aware of how much they have and therefore how little they need. Through realizing their place in the universe, something different is earned: patience.

Artists attempt to cultivate this discreet skill in the midst of working hard for years to conceptualize, perform, and produce. We are told that the harder we work, the closer we will come to our goal. If I spend six hours a day in the practice room, or work fourteen hours in the studio, I demonstrate my devotion. The work takes time and patience. But this idea of "time and patience" is in itself questionable. Composer Marcos Balter relates how he spent a year slowing down, moving and working at a "normal" pace, only to find out that this rhythm didn't work for him. Once he went back to his faster, busier pace he was "exhausted . . . but more complete."

Likewise, gratitude is sticky terrain, especially when hoping to reframe failure and despair. Does everything have a silver lining?

Should we be expected to give thanks for injustice? Activist and writer Angela Davis: "The idea of freedom is inspiring. But what does it mean? If you are free in a political sense but have no food, what's that? The freedom to starve?" What if we lose our jobs or are taken from our families? Is it fair to be asked to give thanks for illness or physical injury?

It is poignant to imagine that we could die with no regrets, that we could find gratitude in the face of whatever challenges we face. But is this even remotely possible? Some don't have that choice. While it is troubling to look at limitation and death—to acknowledge that there will be a time when we and our loved ones will expire—can we imagine that someday we might let go of the fears associated with them? *Ich Habe Genug* summons these kinds of existential questions. Bach acknowledges both pain and gratitude in the cantata's outer Arias, written in minor keys with turgid rhythmic motion. Perhaps he grappled with his own relationship to death while working with the text.

Is it worth naming the gifts in our lives, daily, no matter how small? Will we find peace? Is it worth always searching for answers to our incomplete lives even in the face of constant disappointment? Will it calm us? Is it worth reaffirming the patience to keep going no matter what through great adversity?

No one holds a universal formula. Emotional attachments to people and experiences often obscure my ability to see the abundance in my own life. But maybe, in the morning or evening hours, in the flash of a breakthrough, saying thanks pierces the web of worry. A child is well again. A student is released from prison. Enough. A friend comes home. A chord is found. Perhaps, it is enough.

what I didn't bury

With no performances in sight, it seems ok to leave my violin in its case.

Until now, my rehearsal, playing, and teaching schedule has been relentless. In observation of the shelter-in-place orders, I stay in my apartment and talk to family members for hours, something I have not been able to do in years. We are in good health, fortunately have a little money saved up, and take each strange day as it comes. Despite the very real possibility that my partner and I will both be without jobs or freelance income, we make the best of it. I am both horrified by the unfolding health situation and grateful for the break.

I go about my days without the activity that used to be the most centering: practicing the violin. It is liberating. Every day I sit alone by the window and write many pages by hand in my notebook. After flipping through cookbooks, planning meals and dance parties, I spend time with my children who are in school online, all without worrying about how any of this will take away from my musical work. So much time to think. Everything has shifted and there is nothing else to do.

After a few months I stop considering practicing entirely because it is out of my daily schedule. The violin, sitting untouched in its case underneath our piano, begins to seem like part of my distant past, not the living, breathing wooden body that has commanded my attention for decades.

———⌐∘

I post two questions for the musicians in the chat: 1. What will you hold onto from this current life without performances? 2. What will you discard? It is a workshop for a professional training program, and I am supposed to be talking about forging new career paths. But this is the fall of 2020, we are maybe or maybe not still in the height of the pandemic, and the whole idea of a career in the arts will never be the same. Even though I have navigated the profession for longer, these younger musicians seem better equipped than I to handle a post-pandemic reality.

The responses to the first question are varied. Things to hold onto: quiet and unrestricted time, planned online dates with friends and family, calm stemming from lack of control. The responses to the second question show other sides of the same situation. What to discard: too much unstructured time, spending most days entirely on a computer, the uncertainty of the moment.

The hardest thing, they say, is not performing. Listlessness, feelings of worthlessness—why are we doing what we do if no one is listening? "Do you have a secret to making it through?" they ask me. I share a few half-hearted thoughts. By the end of the workshop, everyone seems to think concerts will return in due time. Even though no one expresses concern about pursuing a career that is presently decimated, it has to be on their minds.

I have few words of advice for these exceptional young players because I too am struggling.

It's an odd mixture of freedom and loss. In walks and runs along the Hudson River, I examine how much I miss the physical act of playing, of using my hands all day to make something. Even the soreness in my limbs that necessitates stretching after practicing, and the mental tiredness that comes from wrestling with a musical text. I miss the satisfaction of working through problems, of figuring out ways to improve—this has been my daily work for over thirty-five years.

And yet I still do not play. I barely touch the instrument besides demonstrating in online violin lessons. Sometimes the bow skates across the violin strings, and I can't engage my sound. It feels like trying to speak again after weeks of silence. Why am I ok with this—is it self-sabotage? Perhaps it is fascination; I am curious to see how long I can last without the routine of music.

A friend argues that creating art isn't an essential activity. Even though I have always defended the position that the arts are critical for human functionality, technically speaking, I can't help wondering if I should reassess. I am alive and even thriving. How can one realistically compare the need for food and shelter with the need to play the violin? Faced with the global health crisis and the function of "essential" workers in our society, I start questioning where the practice and enjoyment of art fits into the picture.

Walking alongside the Hudson on a blustery day, I contemplate whether or not I should give up music for good. I wonder what this might do to me, to my physical and emotional well-being. Does the audience really need the music as much as the musicians do? Maybe it is only about the rush of playing, of performing with others. And now that we are experiencing a life and death situation in a pandemic, maybe we are kidding ourselves that pre-pandemic artistic work as a vocation made a difference to the population as a whole.

I can't remember what it feels like to make music for people, to create sound in space with others. The tenderness of catching each other's eyes onstage. The feeling of full participation from an audience in close proximity. The adrenaline of expressive risk.

Whenever I hear music of any kind, I mirror playing it on the violin, fingering the notes on a piece of paper or on the car steering wheel. I have always taken this automatic response for granted. My heart tries to tug itself out of my body when I hear music that I love. I sob through cantatas by J. S. Bach. I put on an LP of Johannes Brahms's G Major Sextet and lie down to feel the music vibrating through the floor.

A few days of playing through old favorites like the Bach Chaconne or Alban Berg's Violin Concerto never lasts. And begging my children to play duos with me isn't wise for maintaining a somewhat hands-off approach to their musical lives. Attempts at new projects come and go.

As the callouses on my left hand soften and peel off, there are very few remnants of my performance life left. I am burying a part of myself. If my wooden instrument is an appendage, I am laying that phantom limb to rest.

———⌒౨

During one of the many long pandemic days, lingering in thought, I recall an incident early in my life . . .

In my backyard I buried a crayfish. Actually two. My parents had been entreated by the owners of a local restaurant to take these fish home. They saw the pleading eyes of me and my sister after the restaurant's offer, and my parents, ever the kind patrons who had trouble saying no, couldn't refuse the free pets.

We had never owned a fish, so after dropping us at home my father immediately drove to the pet store for research, returning with a basic fish tank and some fish food. We read about how we needed to purify the water in the fish tank, which in the mid-80s involved dumping powder into the tank and swirling it around. We gently released the crayfish from their water bags into the tank and watched them swim in their new environment.

Right away we knew something was wrong. The smaller fish looked to us like it was swollen, bulging as it swam slowly. It reminded me of manatees we had seen while paddling a canoe on a nature reserve in Florida, except in miniature. Waddling through the water, it was listless in comparison to its healthy partner. Eventually my sister and I went to bed, but not before saying a desperate prayer for our new companions.

In the morning we awoke to the news that the smaller fish had died in the night. Gazing at the belly-up animal in the tank, my mother had discovered that the bulge was many bulges: the crayfish was pregnant, bursting with tiny bodies. This explained the owners' eagerness to give her away. What restaurant wanted to serve a pregnant crayfish? Given this track record we wondered if something might befall the other fish as well.

Both frustrated and intrigued by this turn of events, my sister and I prepared a small grave in the backyard (isn't that what one did in these situations?). With a spade we dug out a patch of grass and made a dirt hole big enough for a fish body, even though fate would also deliver the second crayfish to our burial efforts two days later. So much for free pets and alleged 1980s tank purification. We placed a stone over the mini grave so that we would know to avoid the spot when mowing the lawn or erecting badminton nets.

I was annoyed at my parents' inability to adequately protect us from this bad situation. In fairness, they hadn't known prior to that evening what a live crayfish looked like, and none of us would have been able to identify a pregnant one. But the restaurant owners knew, and they had genuinely taken advantage of my parents' good will. The spindly sea creatures never stood a chance in our home.

———⌒⌒———

Even though my distance to the violin is most likely temporary, I have to wonder if I will ever reclaim my attachment to the instrument. These pandemic days obscure my physical need for an expressive outlet. There is too much in the way.

I am haunted by the dilemma of intrinsic versus extrinsic motivation. Without concerts, I, like so many others, lose my will to work and question my place in the world. Where is the integrity in always needing a goal, one of which is money? And since there are no gigs, and no money, shouldn't every artist's intrinsic motivation to play and create rise up—isn't this why we chose this profession in the first place? Performers eye their colleagues from afar, wondering the same things: "Are you practicing at all, and if so, what makes you different? Am I less serious than others—should I need gigs to find artistic relevance?"

Friends of mine philosophize openly on social media about this struggle. They share their annoyance with others who because of circumstance are able to practice, or who have live concerts in other countries. Then they share their shame at this jealousy. They feel guilty about not wanting to go back to full schedules when the pandemic ends. An artistic life demands so much. I confess to friends who are, like me, surviving without concerts, who are relishing in the open time. Others tell of their steps to pursue different professions, open new businesses, enroll in continuing education for new skills. I search for my role in this order.

One afternoon I check my email while sitting on the couch helping a child with a school assignment. In a stream of new messages lies an invite to play concerts the following month in a socially distanced setting. I literally yell, jumping up from the couch and knocking my computer onto the floor.

So much for toying with my identity as a musician and the relevance of art in general, questioning if it is only habit that keeps bringing me back to music, instead of full-bodied involvement. Heart racing, I run through my apartment to my music library. Do I already own the repertoire we will be playing? It doesn't matter—I will find it. As I scan the music quickly I feel a twinge of fear. When we meet for rehearsals will everyone else have improved while I have stagnated? I pull my violin case out from underneath the piano to get started. Here is my beloved instrument, ready to be used once again.

After taking my violin out of its worn satin bag, I run my left hand along its smooth wooden neck. The metal strings shine bright and clear over the black ebony fingerboard. There is no white dust from rosin lingering on the strings or wood—it has been so long. My instrument is light in my hands as I gently grasp the neck of the violin to nestle it between my own neck and shoulder. With the instrument resting under my chin I pluck the strings with my left hand to hear a familiar resonance. Close to my ear again, the sound is foreign but lovely, like an old friend's ringing laughter.

I coat the hair of the bow slowly with new rosin and imagine I am enlivening each hair follicle with the sticky tree sap. A teacher once admonished me to take more care when applying rosin: "You have to massage the teeth of the hair. The whole bow will sharpen and sing in response." The more intentionally I put on the rosin, the more clarity I will achieve when playing.

I raise both bow and violin to tune the open strings. The sound is gloriously sincere, a reminder of how this violin and I bonded to one another years ago. The vibrations feel like air on my skin. I bend my knees and open my shoulders to start playing a movement from a solo Bach Sonata.

But the strings cut into my now soft fingertips, and I wince. My sensitive nerve endings bristle; I will need to build up my callouses again. What an odd feeling, to know this instrument like a part of my own body but to be so unprepared to use it. I go back to playing the open strings, focusing on the basic resonance of the violin. This will take time.

In that moment I am connected to all of the people before me who have also chosen music. After all of the fear and hatred and death brought about by the pandemic, I know that I will continue to pursue this work. It is work, and there is a way forward.

———

I have read too many articles about the death of classical music and lack of appreciation of fine art in general to take them seriously. Their fearmongering tones are predictable and unhelpful, except when justifying the dismantling of harmful practices. The articles come out; arts administrators rush in to show competing data and evidence of successful audience growth, engaged young people and increased ticket sales; then we go about our lives. The artists mostly shrug off the concern—we adapt to changing needs, reach out to audiences, and welcome people to our events. The cycle is not new.

What is new is the chance performers of all disciplines have to respond to this unique crisis. Italian philosopher Franco "Bifo" Berardi mused at the beginning of the pandemic that in the aftermath humans might associate the automated world with infection and disease. Since we had been forced to exchange being with each other for squinting into a computer, at the end of the nightmare we would view our online worlds as confined and unappealing; leave our phones at home while walking through the park holding a friend's hand; write a letter instead of a text to explain our deepest feelings; choose to touch and live in the flesh.

In reckoning with our fears and worries we will decide to meet each other in space once again, to engage with those who are hungry for what they have missed, for what performers have to give in abundance, for what we thought we had to bury.

notes for themselves

PRESENCE

(for my children: shapeshifters, creators, persons outside the binary)

Uncommon stillness occurs in a space when people enter into vulnerability. The way a group engages can be palpable, unfocused, resistant, immersive, complete. A rare form of intimacy.

Ludwig van Beethoven: Op. 132 string quartet at Nebraska State Penitentiary

We have been instructed to bring only our instruments, an ID, and car keys, and wear simple pants and long-sleeved tops. My string quartet waits in line to go through a rigorous security check. We wonder how we will be received.

The two groups are differentiated by the level of security: medium and maximum. In addition to playing music by Dmitry Shostakovich and Gabriela Lena Frank, we are also performing the slow movement from Ludwig van Beethoven's Op. 132 quartet, a twenty-minute-long hymn of thanksgiving written after the composer's hard-won journey from sickness to convalescence. We worried that it might be too long, the immersive series of chorales too intense for listeners unaccustomed to this music.

One bald, heavily tattooed man in the front row leans in as we play our softest moment; two other men in front lean backwards in their chairs, eyes closed. Their deep listening is evident in the held energy of their bodies. Other men are taking careful note of our slightest interactions with each other, following a look between the second violinist and cellist, moving slightly with the music's rhythm.

Almost all of the men stay after the concert to talk about the music. A man with long black hair pulled into a ponytail empathizes with Beethoven's predicament. Others nod. The bald man says he wishes someone would teach him violin in prison. I move instinctively to give him my violin and bow to play, but then remember we are not allowed any physical contact.

Who has or gives or is allowed the time or opportunity to be present?

Alfonso Cuaron: Roma

The sound of water emerges slowly from the darkness. At first we cannot tell how far away it is. Then it begins to overtake the space, oozing through the curtains of the theater, gurgling up from beneath the floor. That delicious water sound. The large screen suddenly reveals liquid sumptuously washing back and forth across black and white checkered tiles. Playful liquid in a theater full of people breathing dry and thin so they won't be heard.

We start dissolving into the water. Where is it? In what situation would there be so much water on top of black and white checkered tiles? Is the whole film in black and white? How long have we been watching the water wash over the tile squares?

A tiny plane flies overhead, reflected in the pool. It looks impossibly small, like a delicate figurine. The water continues passing by, making ripples and waves upon itself.

We circle around the drain, we glide along the floor. We wash back and forth in a motion we now accept as routine, in a rhythm we know and remember. The liquid creates space for us to become its presence.

John Cage: 4'33"

The piece of music commences with the timer. Holding violin and bow in hand, sitting still in the white-walled classroom, I listen. We all listen.

The woman in the corner with dark green eyeshadow, chain earrings, and immaculate hair drops a plastic fork, she rustles her takeout bags. She stops, embarrassed, looks down. The man with a thick beard who asked five questions at the beginning of class rests his chin on his hands and folds inward.

Faint music with a beat passes by in the hallway outside. It subsides. People breathe out. They look around and settle in. Tightness in the air softens. We are now a group. My steady pulse vibrates through the wood of my violin as I hold my instrument. At four minutes and thirty-three seconds the piece is over.

Afterwards, one student shares their panic; another fears that she missed something, a direction. Why wasn't the performer "doing anything"? What were we listening to?

A few answers: noise, the hums of the room, private sounds.

And the decades-old question: is this listening called music? No one said it *wasn't* music. These visual art students aren't interested in labels. They think we are listening to a sound-art piece from the 1950s. They claim they have seen everything, that John Cage's *Four Minutes and Thirty-Three Seconds* isn't so radical.

But isn't this proof, I argue as their class guest, that art has the capacity to manipulate the pace at which we live? Art's power is literally extraordinary. It can catch us off guard, demand that we ponder, that we grieve, that we squirm, that we wait.

To taste a room, to be truly in now. Presence might pass us by.

acknowledgments

This book began in an uncertain time in my life, when I had just moved back to New York City, was changing professional affiliations, and had few gigs. In the absence of much professional musical work, I started writing about memorization and nostalgia and kept going. I am immensely grateful to Joy Castro for believing in my writing and encouraging the existence of this collection. Huge thanks to Becca Bostock for her perceptive close reading and editing, and to Kristen Elias Rowley, Samara Rafert, Tara Cyphers, Juliet Williams, Kristina Wheeler, and everyone at The Ohio State University Press for their work publishing this book. Much gratitude to Regina Starace for her gorgeous cover design.

I am indebted to the following people who were involved in crucial stages of this manuscript. To Giancarlo Latta and Lisa Bielawa, two of my first readers, both of whose insights were immeasurably helpful to me. Many thanks to Tricia Park and Colleen Jennings for reading and discussing early drafts of essays, and to Jennifer Tarlin, Joan Allison, Susan Gottschalk, Deborah Sherr, Carla Ness, Abigail Fischer, Rachel Noyes, Ania Szary-Berkowitz, and Hannah Collins for their conversations. Thanks to Kanan

Patel and Angelina Hawley-Dolan at Aster Montessori School for letting me invent a writing residency in their beautiful space when I needed it most, and to the Adler family, who welcomed me into their home for quiet editing time.

Thank you to all of my mentors and teachers over the years, some of whose life-changing contributions I have attempted to honor in this book.

While this is not a book about the Chiara Quartet, so much of my life for eighteen years was devoted to working with these three incredible people—Hyeyung Sol Yoon, Jonah Sirota, and Gregory Beaver—and I am forever grateful to you for our experiences together.

Likewise, huge gratitude and love for my extended family and how they continue to shape and support my life, especially: Abigail, Jeanne, Norman, Jason, Barbara, Steve, Vincent, Elizabeth, Angelina, Chris, Erika, Katie, and those who are no longer with us.

This book could not have happened without my two children guiding, challenging, and inspiring me along the way. I love you Oriana and Ilaria.

And to my partner in all things who reads and addresses everything with the most innovative and critical lens, who holds me accountable, and in whose eyes I am my best self—thank you Anthony for our extraordinary love and life together.

MACHETE

Joy Castro, Series Editor

This series showcases fresh stories, innovative forms, and books that break new aesthetic ground in nonfiction—memoir, personal and lyric essay, literary journalism, cultural meditations, short shorts, hybrid essays, graphic pieces, and more—from authors whose writing has historically been marginalized, ignored, and passed over. The series is explicitly interested in not only ethnic and racial diversity, but also gender and sexual diversity, neurodiversity, physical diversity, religious diversity, cultural diversity, and diversity in all of its manifestations. The machete enables path-clearing; it hacks new trails and carves out new directions. The Machete series celebrates and shepherds unique new voices into publication, providing a platform for writers whose work intervenes in dangerous ways.